BUCKSHOT PIE

A Family's Struggle Through Homesteading, The Great Depression, and World War II

BUCKSHOT PIE

A Family's Struggle Through Homesteading, The Great Depression, and World War II

CHRIS GREGORY

SEMPER PI PUBLISHING
TEKOA, WASHINGTON

BUCKSHOT PIE

*A Family's Struggle Through Homesteading,
The Great Depression, and World War II*

Published by Semper Pi Publishing
535 North Madison Street
Tekoa, Washington 99033
www.BuckshotPie.com

First Edition 2013
Printed in the United States

ISBN: 978-09895294-0-2 (Hardcover)
ISBN: 978-09895294-1-9 (Paperback)
ISBN: 978-09895294-2-6 (ebook)
ISBN: 978-09895294-3-3 (ePub)

Library of Congress Control Number: 2013909919

Copyediting and Typesetting by All My Best
www.AllMyBest.com

Cover and Website Design by Monkey C Media
www.MonkeyCMedia.com

For the next generation

Madeline Marie

Trenton Eugene

and

Ella Joyce

CONTENTS

ILLUSTRATIONS

FOREWORD

As I stood at the kitchen stove that spring morning, the thought from long ago was passing through my mind yet again. I should write a story of the many struggles of this family. I first considered this 55 years ago at age ten after looking through the material I had found in a dresser drawer. There were newspaper clippings, photographs, telegrams, postcards, awards, documents, souvenirs, birth certificates, memorial records, and letters. They told of a tough time homesteading on marginal land, early deaths, survival through difficult economic times in the 1930s, and World War II experiences. Those war experiences included two near-death crash landings, the Bataan Death March, and both Japanese and Nazi prison camps. Ever since the time I first read that material, I've had a keen interest in homesteading, The Great Depression, and World War II. I had a background of studying those topics in school at Oakesdale and later in college. I had experience teaching about those subjects over a 34-year career in education. It was a story worth telling; and with my background, all that material, the oral history of uncles and an aunt, and my father's copious and vivid memories, I should be able to write that book.

Oops, one of the eggs spilled out on the warm stove top as I cracked it—get a rag and clean it up before it starts to cook. The bacon was starting to burn—get the tongs! Just then the toast popped up and I had to flip it over because the toaster, after a mere 3 years, only toasted on one side. Aahhh! Another breakfast gone wrong! That happens about half the time for me with breakfast or just about anything else. How did I think I could write this story? But my father and his brothers had experienced unique lives. He is

90 and all his siblings have passed away. If their story is to be told, I'm probably the only one who can do it.

Those five brothers were part of Tom Brokaw's "greatest generation." They started life on a scabrock farm, survived The Great Depression, and were instrumental in World War II. But how could I have the audacity to write their story?

I was reminded of another morning a few years ago, one that I fouled up at a 4:00 a.m. breakfast—getting ready to take my grandson fishing. It was going to be a cold opening day float-tube fly-fishing at Dry Falls Lake. We would need a thermos of hot tea. I heated the water on high, put in several Constant Comment tea bags, and the tags flopped over the side and onto the electric eye. Oops, I've got fire in the kitchen. Still in an early morning mental fog, I quickly grabbed a dish towel to snuff out the fire, but the towel burst into flames. Finally, I got water on it and put out all the flames, but by that time the smoke detector was blowing annoyingly loud. The wife and grandson were up and wondering what was going on.

Thinking of that morning, I asked myself once again: Could I actually write this story? I've accomplished a few things, some remarkable and some regrettable, but about half the time I'd screw things up. Everything's been a 50-50 proposition with me. Could I do this? I should at least try. Brokaw urged others to write about that generation because there were certainly other stories worth telling. With the early loss of a father, those boys—my dad and uncles, at ages one through ten, had certainly had a tough life—especially surviving the war and then returning to civilian life and trying to have normal family lives.

On one hand, I'm not a writer. I had to work hard to get C's in my college writing classes. But now I had the time to write. After being involved in public education for 34 years, teaching mostly history, I had fully retired 4 years ago. I'd hunted pheasants at all my favorite spots in Whitman County with my childhood friend Roy Anderson. We always had my Brittany spaniel, Rebbie, and my

English setter, Steptoe Butte's Buddy. We enjoyed harvesting pheasants and partridge, but most of all we marveled at the dogs' robust work and staunch points. Also, I'd fished at all the favorite childhood spots like Williams, Badger, Rock, Amber, Clear, Fish, Benewah, and Fishtrap lakes, as well as the Snake, San Poil, Kettle, and St. Joe rivers and Black Creek. But you can't hunt and fish every day. My wife and I couldn't afford to play bingo at the Coeur d'Alene Casino more than a couple of times a month. Sure, we could drive to Spokane for an occasional dinner and a movie. The grandkids had moved out, and although I had to occasionally chauffeur them around for sports, music lessons, shopping, camps, doctor appointments, etc., I still had an abundance of time.

I decided to do it!

Prologue

Vigil for Neva

We weep over the graves of infants and the little ones taken from us by death, but an early grave may be the shortest path to heaven.

—Tryon Edwards

April 28, 2013 was a beautiful day in eastern Washington State. The winter wheat was filling the Palouse Hills of northeastern Whitman County with a deep verdant covering. A light breeze caught the feathery young shoots, and this pleasant green blanket of growth undulated across the dune-shaped hills like gentle waves on the Snake River. Earlier in the morning I had left our Tekoa Mountain home and traveled the 12 miles southwest to the small farming community of Oakesdale. My son and eldest granddaughter had traveled about the same distance southeast from Rosalia. There, at my parents' home of 60 years, I picked up Trevor and Madeline, along with my dad, Delbert. We were headed 55 miles southwest to the Winona Community Cemetery. In the back of my Jeep Cherokee rested a granite headstone recently finished by my dad's neighbor and stone smith, Bob Hooper. Bob had carved the stone and, he wanted to donate it for this purpose. We were going to place it on the unmarked grave of my dad's sister, Neva Lavelle.

As usual, Delbert was talkative, but not about the task at hand. I usually had to pry some details from him, especially those about his childhood, the homestead... the war. He often talked freely about relatives, but usually about those many local ancestors and relatives on my mother's side of the family—the Halls, Littletons, Millers, Shahans, Burkes, Willsons, Durhams, Hardins, Gallahers, Ingrams, Crows, and many more. Most had come from Tennessee between 1890 and 1910. Most of them were farmers, and many still lived around the old homesteads near Tennessee Flats, Cashup Flats, Steptoe, St. John, Colfax, Rosalia, Tekoa, and Oakesdale. This was some of the richest farm country in the world. Wheat, barley, peas, and lentils, but wheat was the mainstay crop. And the wheat provided a lucrative bounty for many.

However, the land farther west around the old Gregory homestead was less productive. The homestead was marginal land. It gave a hardy challenge even to the most industrious of farm workers. It was much drier, most of it had thinner topsoil, and some of it was scabland scoured by ancient floods... scoured down to the volcanic basalt rock.

We passed through the small farming community of Sunset with its four or five houses, and next, St. John with its attempt at community revival. Then somewhere between St. John and Ewan we began to see changes in the countryside. It was drier with more exposed basalt cliffs, rock outcrops, gullies, and ravines. The wind was more prevalent here, with strong dust-laden gusts and little dust devils. As we turned south on Cherry Creek Road, we could see the stark difference. On the east side of the road were the beautiful rolling hills of the Palouse; and on the west side, rugged, stark scabland with little or no soil. "There goes one," Delbert remarked. The ring-neck pheasant launched itself from the hill on the left where it had been scratching for kernels of grain. It quickly beat its wings a few times, set its wings, and glided about 200 yards to the gulley on our right. "It'll be another good season," he barely whispered, subtly exposing the fact that his hunting days were over.

As the road veered to the southwest, we could see Big Cove Canyon, a deep, U-shaped trench with jagged, hackly basalt floor, steep walls of columnar basalt, and talus slopes. We then followed the winding Palouse River to the remnants of the small community of Winona. Slowing down, we observed a couple of grain elevators and grain storage warehouses, a half dozen homes, the derelict remains of a few stores, and a smattering of outbuildings fallen in on themselves. From there we traveled a mile west to the Winona Community Cemetery.

The headstone must have had some deep-down meaning for us and only us. Neva was born a century earlier, on May 14, 1914. She was the first child of Charles Ralph Gregory and Lucinda Pearl Johnson Gregory. Neva was a healthy, happy, energetic, beautiful little girl. However, her second winter was harsh and the following spring brought dust and continuous winds. She had bronchitis, high fevers, abdominal pain, and distension. Sadly, Charles and Pearl's first born didn't survive the maladies. Neva passed away a few days short of her second birthday. Of course, Delbert never really knew Neva, since he was born 7 years after her death. And Neva never had the opportunity to know the world; but worse yet, the world and the people of Winona and Whitman County never got the chance to know her.

That's how the family started—with a tear and a stifled whimper. There were many more sorrows and some joys, but mostly a struggle—a struggle to survive and prosper. Pearl washed Neva's body. She then wrapped her lifeless little girl in clean white clothing and a soft, white linen blanket. She carried little Neva in her arms as Charles hitched the mules to the town wagon and drove the six long, hard miles to the Winona cemetery. They buried her and placed a wooden cross—the cross Charles had fashioned and on which he had whittled the name Neva Gregory the previous night—a sleepless night of deep pain and many tears.

On Memorial Day of 1957, 41 years after that burial, our family traveled to Winona and proceeded to the Gregory section of the Winona cemetery. Delbert placed flowers on the graves of his parents, Neva, and William, his paternal grandfather. Neva's wooden cross had rotted and fallen into pieces. Delbert replaced it with a temporary marker of steel rebar. I suggested that we needed to bring Neva a stone and Delbert replied, "We'll try to do that someday." Nonetheless, life gets in the way; things keep us occupied and life slows us down. But finally, 56 years after that promise, we had arrived at the cemetery with her newly fashioned headstone. Delbert was silent now and ready to place the marker in the dust next to the graves of his parents, Charles Ralph and Lucinda Pearl; his grandfather William Thomas; Delbert's sister Juanita Arline "Nita"; and her husband, Howard Vernon Long.

As I looked around, I recognized the cemetery's surroundings from years earlier. There was windswept land with dry sagebrush, some bunch grass, rock outcrops of scabland, but mostly dry, powdery soil. This is the area where my dad had been born almost 90 years earlier. It is a tough, hard-bitten land with some marginal soil—soil productive only in the very best of years, the years with sufficient rainfall, average wind, and good health for those who farmed it. This is the story of a 1910 farm family with pioneer spirit, hope in a homestead, pride, intelligence, and a century of challenges lying before them.

Chapter 1

The Move to Washington State

The dark mold is upturned
By the sharp-pointed plow;
And I've a lesson learned.

My life is but a field
Stretched out beneath God's sky
Some harvest rich to yield.

Where grows the golden grain?
Where faith? Where sympathy?
In a furrow cut by pain.

—Maltbie D. Babcock

An imposing 6'4" figure, William Thomas Gregory at age 46 stood at the head of the kitchen table on his late father-in-law's farm near Hutchinson, Kansas. The year was 1910. At the table sat his adult children: 24-year-old Guy Thomas and wife Vesta, 22-year-old Ella Belle, 20-year-old Earl Farold, and 19-year-old Charles Ralph. Two days earlier they had put their mother, William's wife, Mary Joyce Mourn Gregory, to rest. She had passed away from rheumatic fever at age 50. Her younger brothers were taking over the operation of the Mourn family farm. That's the way things were done back then. William and his children had their future to plan.

As they considered options, the decision was made to stay together. Ella Belle had worked for a telephone company in

Hutchinson and she had a close circle of friends in that city, but she felt it more important to stay with her father and brothers. Guy had worked for a railroad company, first as a laborer and most recently as a maintenance supervisor. He felt that he could get a similar well-paying position wherever the family relocated. Earl and Charles each wanted to work their own farms. That had been the life of both boys, and they loved to work the soil and bring forth crops. For the past decade they had worked on their grandfather Mourn's farm. They had harvested timber and raised hogs, chickens, and dairy and beef cattle, but mainly they had grown alfalfa, oats, barley, and, most importantly, wheat. Now, the family was studying government pamphlets and railroad brochures. The most promising prospect appeared to be homesteading in eastern Washington — Whitman County looked like the land of milk and honey.

At age 21, a farmer could file for a half section of land, pay a $16.00 fee, improve the land, and 5 years later receive the title free and clear. Whitman County on the Columbia Plateau seemed ideal. Kansas was the leading wheat-growing state in the country, but Whitman County was the leading wheat-producing county in the nation. Charles was certain he wanted to continue as a wheat farmer, but he was too young to homestead. They decided that William would homestead a farm for Charles, and then Earl would assist them. After that farm was established, Earl would homestead and they would, in turn, help him make improvements. Guy would get a railroad position nearby and help in his spare time. Also, Ella would get a telephone operator's position nearby, and she would assist the brothers. All were in agreement.

Arrangements were made and they obtained their homestead in Texas Draw, near Winona, Washington. The town of Winona was a small community in western Whitman County. The town was named by a railroad worker who was surveying for the Columbia and Palouse Railway in 1882. The surveyor chose the name because he came from Winona, Minnesota and was homesick for his medium-sized hometown. Of course the towns were much different in size. The 1900 population of Winona, Minnesota was 19,714. But the diminutive farming community of Winona, Washington was one hundredth that size, with a population of approximately 200.

Winona, Washington was about 7 miles south by southeast of the homestead. The homestead was near the Palouse Hills with the world's richest soil. But it was farther west in a drier microclimate among the channeled scablands, some of the poorest ground in the northwest. It was bordering the two land forms and was thus marginal farmland—lucrative during years with abundant rainfall and very hard labor, but questionable during drier years.

They established a respectable farm in this Winona country. They built a two-story house, constructed a cistern on the nearby west hummock, and erected a windmill to pump water to the cistern. This allowed indoor plumbing, but of course they built an outhouse as well. The cistern and windmill also provided water for the livestock watering troughs. They purchased some mules and farm equipment and began tilling the soil. Within 2 years, Charles's small holding was beginning to prosper. He also met, courted, and married Pearl Johnson from Walla Walla. She had been employed as a mid-nurse for Dr. D. W. Henry in nearby Endicott.

Guy acquired another railroad supervisory job. This one was with the Milwaukee Railway at Revere, only a few miles north of the homestead. Guy and Vesta resided in nearby Rock Lake, where they brought their fifth child, little Theada Belle, into the world. However, when the railroad was constructed 2 miles south of there, everyone in Rock Lake disassembled their homes, outbuildings, and stores and reassembled them about 2 miles south at Ewan, a town named in honor of the primary property owners, the Russian-born, German-Americans Mr. and Mrs. Willis Anson Evans.

In following years as Guy earned railroad promotions, he and Vesta transferred to Lind in Adams County, then to St. Maries, along the St. Joe River in Benewah County, Idaho, and finally to Metaline Falls, Pend Oreille County, Washington. They raised nine children:

William, Francis, Edith, Esther, Theada Belle, Dale, Lester, Leonard, and Verda. Like his younger brother Charles, Guy would also have four sons serve in World War II.

After Earl turned 21, he homesteaded his half section of farmland. He wasn't able to obtain wheat farmland in the Whitman County area. However, he did acquire some good sandy loam farmland at the area known as Hanford Reach, about 70 miles west of the Winona homestead and bordering the Columbia River on the west side. This land was too arid for the dry farming techniques of wheat, but through irrigation he was able to establish a substantial mint farm. Like Charles, Earl kept half his land in fallow. That is, half the land was planted and harvested, while the other half was tilled and weeded, but remained unplanted for a time. That way the nutrients were replenished when allowed to sit fallow.

With mint contracts from Wrigley's of Chicago, and Imperial Corporation's Society Candies of Seattle, he was able to make a lucrative living on this farm. However, the federal government wanted that land for top secret research. Originally, the land may have been obtained for chemical weapons research, but years later it became part of the Hanford Nuclear Reservation. Earl was informed that through the law of eminent domain the government would confiscate the land, but he would be reimbursed a sum of money based on the value of the land and its production capacity.

Earl was able to invest this money while moving to the vacated home of Guy and Vesta in Ewan. Earl then helped his younger brother Charles and father William on the Winona homestead. It was at about this time that Earl met, courted, and wedded Estella Pless of Sprague, Washington. In 1918, they had twin boys, Delvin Eugene and Melvin Eugene. For a variety of reasons, infant mortality was still high in the early Twentieth Century—ten times today's rate, but it was no less heartbreaking for Stella and Earl when they lost baby Del within the month on May 18, 1918, and little Mel 2 years later on April 4, 1920. At this time there was a world-wide epidemic of Spanish flu, and it was so serious that millions had perished from that virulent influenza. This may have been the cause of the boys' deaths, but pernicious childhood diseases were also ubiquitous with very little effective medication. Earl and Stella buried their twin boys at the cemetery near St. John and eventually moved on to use their investments to purchase land in the shadow of Mt. Rainier in western Washington. Their ranch was a diversified concern, harvesting timber, raising dairy and beef cattle, as well as growing a few crops. They had two more children whom they raised to adulthood: Farold Eugene and Harold Laverne.

Ella Belle enjoyed her work at the telephone company, but she missed her old circle of friends back in Hutchinson, Kansas. She penned letters to them often, especially her closest friend Minerva Madeline Menzie. Minerva had married their mutual friend John Upton Menzie. Ella was thrilled for Minerva when she shared the news of her pregnancy and forthcoming birth. They corresponded often to keep up with each other's activities, especially the excitement of the baby that Minerva would soon have. However, at about the anticipated time of the birth, Ella received no more letters from her friend. Ella composed several unanswered letters, but after about a month she received a heart-wrenching message from John: While they had been blessed with Kenneth, a healthy baby boy, Ella's friend Minerva had died in childbirth. Ella and John exchanged letters over the next few months, and John eventually asked Ella to betroth, return to Kansas, marry, and help him raise Kenneth. This request was unexpected, but Ella felt it was the correct and natural thing to do. She had known John most of her life and considered him to be an industrious man of sterling character. She also considered it her honor and duty to raise her best friend's son. Within a short time Ella returned to Hutchinson and wedded John.

Over the next few years they had a daughter, Velda Belle; a son, Virgil Leroy; another son, Guy Warren; and a third son, Leonard

Calvin. Ella proudly dedicated her life to raising Kenneth and her four children, always giving each one an equal amount of love and caring. In order to help with income, Ella took in seamstress work at home. John borrowed money to construct a group of grain storage warehouses and elevators. Local wheat farmers paid to store grain in his facilities. He sometimes purchased some of the grain when prices were well below a dollar per bushel and sell when prices hovered around a dollar. They made a lucrative living until the 1930s, when the area experienced a horrific drought coupled with strong winds. This was often referred to as the Dust Bowl, severely affecting 17 of the Midwestern states. John and Ella stuck it out and found ways to survive. John and their son Virgil established an equipment and farm implement outlet in Montezuma, Kansas, eventually converted over to John Deere in 1940, and that business thrived for 70 years.

Although William's family eventually went their separate ways, the Winona wheat farm homestead remained the center of the family for almost two decades. The farm was turned over to Charles Ralph and his wife, Pearl. Charles worked it vigorously and effectively. Working a wheat farm using Hardy Campbell's scientific dry-farming technique is what Charles studied as a young boy. It's what he practiced as a teenager on his maternal grandfather's farm. And now he was proud to work diligently almost every day for his farm and the future of his family.

Downtown Winona, Whitman County, Washington State about 1910.

L–R: Pearl Johnson at age 16, the 2 nurse instructors, Lyman Charles Johnson, and Charles Lyman Johnson on buggy, mid-nurse training, Walla Walla, Washington, 1910.

William with first grandchild,
William, 1913.

Earl Farold and Estella
Pless Gregory, 1916.

L–R: Ella Belle, Velda Belle, Virgil, Kenneth, Guy Warren, and John
Menzie, Kansas, 1922.

Charles Ralph and Pearl Johnson Gregory, Winona, Whitman County, Washington, 1912.

Chapter 2

The Farm and Family of
Charles and Pearl

Of all nature's gifts to the human race, what is sweeter to a man
than his children?

—Marcus Tullius Cicero

Located in northwestern Whitman County just 4 miles east of
Adams County and 16 miles south of Spokane County lies the half
section of land once farmed by Charles Gregory, Sr. Half of one
square mile, it totaled 320 acres. It was a half mile wide from east to
west and a mile deep from north to south. The Jordan-Knott Road
ran east to west along the northern border of the homestead. North
of the road lay the barren scabrock and pothole gulley known as the
west branch of Texas Draw. About a half-mile to the east was Texas
Lake. South of the Jordan-Knott Road the land rose about thirty
degrees to the house and then tapered off in a central plain.

This broad plain rose just a few degrees as it narrowed for about
a half mile to the south. The plain served as pasture land for the
family's livestock. On each side were the land forms the people of
this area referred to as hummocks. The north side of the hummocks
rose about a hundred feet with narrow, sharp-pitched fronts like the
prow of a ship; then, as they ran south, they broadened and declined
at a slight pitch for a mile. On the inside edges of the hummocks, the
sides were steep as well. The tops of these hummocks were flat, with
deep soil and only a slight pitch tilting south. As the two hummocks

decreased in height, the plain rose in altitude so that the three land forms met a half mile south. The tops of the hummocks and the joining of all the three landforms in that southern half mile were variously referred to as tabletop, mesa, or bench land. These south slopes provided arable land that could produce up to fifty bushels of wheat per acre during years that received around 10 inches of annual precipitation.

This is the land upon which Charles worked so hard to produce a lucrative crop of wheat. He used *Campbell's Soil Culture Manual* to study the correct techniques for farming dry or semi-arid land. The manual could be purchased for $2.50. It was professionally bound and covered in soothing, moss-colored cloth. A golden camel was embossed on the front cover, below which were the words, "The Camel for the Sahara Desert—The Campbell Method for the American Desert." The method made it possible to farm these dry lands, but the necessary rigor was almost debilitating. The more arid the land, the more tilling was necessary. The Winona land was arid and required Charles to plow and disc and harrow the land many times in order to make the soil fine enough to hold the available moisture. A popular refrain for some semi-arid land farmers follows:

> *I've started to dry farm*
> *A piece of bench land sod,*
> *And if I meet no harm*
> *I'll win or bust — by jinks.*
> *Plow and harrow and disk —*
> *Disc and harrow and plow:*
> *Of course there is some risk*
> *Until a chap knows how.*
> *Campbell says they will grow*
> *If seeds are put in right —*
> *Depends on how you sow*
> *With ground in proper plight.*
> *And so I work all day:*
> *At night I read this book —*
> *I get no time to play*
> *And hardly time to cook.*

It is doubtful that Charles had time for such refrains or even much time to read. He had his work cut out for him, and he knew what to do. He plowed deep into about 280 acres of the south slopes and waited for rainfall to soak deep into the furrows. Then he applied the disc to the land to break up the furrows, used a spike-toothed harrow to further break up the soil, and finally used a spring-toothed harrow to turn the soil into a fine powdery cover that would prevent evaporation of the accumulated moisture.

He then planted about 140 acres in wheat. The roots of the wheat grew deep to search for the moisture, and by the middle of each July the crop turned golden and ripe for harvest. The other 140 acres of tilled farmland lay dormant during each of these growing cycles in order to allow the nutrients to replenish the soil. Using this summer fallow technique, he rotated the two fields each year, allowing the land to remain rich and fertile.

The harvest almost always took place in late July, when the temperatures often reached 100 degrees. This was grueling labor, especially in the heat. The wheat was cut by hand and placed in the wagon; and when the wagon was full, it was taken to the stationary thresher. Powered by a straw-powered steam engine, the thresher shook and filtered the wheat to separate the kernels. After several trips to and from the field, the town wagon was filled with the golden grain. Then, depending on prices and road conditions, the harvested wheat was taken by wagon either to Winona, about 7 miles to the south, or Revere Siding, approximately 6 miles to the north. On a good year, as much as $5,000 could be grossed, but that was only if Charles worked from daybreak to dusk. However, he also needed his father to work hard during harvest and help him take care of the livestock throughout the year.

The home for the farm was built about 30 yards up the slope from the road and next to the west hummock. The family built a two-story wood framed house. The home had a large front porch, a downstairs bedroom for William, a master bedroom upstairs for

Charles and Pearl, and two smaller upstairs bedrooms. The downstairs living and dining room was large enough when cleared to be used for square dances. When harvest was finished each year, the family hosted a square dance for farm families from the surrounding areas near Endicott, Winona, Revere, Ewan, Lancaster, and Benge.

Next to the home was a windmill that pumped water to the cistern near the top of the west hummock. On the slope below the mill lay an orchard of apple, apricot, and plum trees, as well as a large garden producing many root crops, beans, peas, cabbage, raspberries, and gooseberries.

On the central plain behind the house, the family had erected a horse and cattle barn, two watering troughs, a machine shed, corrals, a chicken coop, a pig barn, a storage shed, and an outhouse. Money had to be borrowed from the Winona Bank in order to purchase the materials, and a great deal of work was required in order to build and erect these structures. Funds were also borrowed to pay for equipment and animals. Equipment included a stationary thresher, a steam engine, plows for both Charles and William, two discs, a global (with larger curved discs, to make furrows smaller than a plow, but larger than a standard disc), a spike-toothed harrow, a spring-toothed harrow, two wagons, a roller or compacter, a rod weeder, a seeder, pitch forks, shovels, standard tools, posts, various types of wire (barbed, chicken, pig, etc.), and harnesses. Animals were also purchased: a work horse, a western riding pony they named Caesar, a half dozen hogs, two dozen chickens, three milking cows they named Bossy, Jersie, and Guernsie, a feeder steer to raise and butcher, and, most importantly, seven mules. Based on his experience in Kansas, Charles said mules were necessary to be successful because they could work all day long. Of course a mule is a cross between a mare horse and a male donkey. Most mules are smaller than a horse, but with five times the stamina. Three of Charles's mules had been the result of a cross with very large draft horses, probably of some Belgium, Percheron, or Clydesdale blood. These mules were enormous and larger than his big workhorse.

They proved to be very effective. They had special efficacy at breaking virgin sod, stubble fields, or rocky soil to the plow.

Everything was in place for a successful wheat farm. After all, the government pamphlets and the railroad brochures from Milwaukee Railway and James J. Hill's Great Northern and Northern Pacific railroads had claimed these homesteads were the land of milk and honey. But of course both the railroads and the government profited from increased population in the northwest and increased shipment of goods to and from this area. Consequently, their claims were somewhat exaggerated, if not downright spurious. Some of the homesteaders in eastern Montana and the Dakotas had an impossible road to success. Although the Winona area had a better microclimate than those regions, it was still much drier than the rest of Whitman County. Also, its soil was not as deep as that of the Palouse Hills. Therefore, in order to hold enough moisture for a rewarding crop, the farmer sometimes had to till the ground twice as many times. This meant that farmers in this western slice of Whitman County often had to start the season earlier and work longer days—sometimes 14-hour days. This was difficult, but Charles relished the challenge, especially with the help of his father and, when possible, his brothers.

With the farm in place and a clear path to success, Charles and Pearl were eager to start a family. Their first baby was delivered on May 14, 1914. Neva Lavelle was a beautiful little girl with an easy smile and plenty of energy. She brought many smiles to their faces, and Grandpa William was equally proud of such a healthy, happy, and active little baby. Little Neva received her first postcard on Christmas Eve, 1915. She was 19 months old. The card was from her Uncle Jewell Waddle (Pearl Johnson Gregory's half-brother) and Aunt Pearl Waddle from Walla Walla. It was addressed to Miss Neva Gregory in care of Chas. Gregory. The stamp displayed the words, "United States of America; Security, Education, Conservation, and Health, postage one cent." On the front of the card were the words, "Wishing you Good Cheer. The best of best wishes for Christmas I send, Good Luck and contentment their brilliancy lend." Also on the front was a picture of a doll in red cape and hood. She was holding a poinsettia and sitting on a basket with holly and a message of "*MERRY CHRISTMAS*." Little Neva pointed to the picture of the doll and said, "That's me."

Little Neva's Christmas postcard, 1915.

She was right! That was her. Neva was a little doll with such a great disposition that she brought joy to those who knew her. However, it was a short, joyous period for Pearl and Charles. Four months after Christmas, Neva had a very high temperature, labored breathing with congestion, and abdominal distress, and she fell into a deep sleep. Pearl kept a cold wet rag on Neva's forehead and gave her sips of water. She wept for her baby, but after three days of this, Neva was gone to the world. The *Colfax Gazette* printed this story:

Buries Little Daughter

Neva, the young daughter of Mr. and Mrs. Charles Gregory, died Tuesday night. The girl had been ill for only a few days, and her death is a great shock to the parents. Neva would have been two years old the 14th of this month. Her death was due to inflammation of the bowels. After eating a little candy last Friday she was taken ill and never regained consciousness. It is not supposed that the candy had anything to do with the disorder. She was the only child.

A funeral was held at the Baptist church Thursday morning and the little one laid to rest in the Winona cemetery. Rev. G. M. Harrington preached the funeral sermon. Many of the neighbors gathered at the church to pay their respects and do anything they could to lighten the sorrow of Mr. and Mrs. Gregory.

Neva Lavelle, 4 months, September 22, 1914.

At this time around the world, trouble was brewing. The problems originated in Europe, which had become increasingly fractionalized and nationalistic. Most of the the European empires and greater nations had alliances that guaranteed protection to smaller states. Many regions had ethnic groups of one country located inside an antagonistic neighboring nation. The area was ripe for a conflagration and just needed a spark to start a war that could spread around the world. That spark occurred in June 1914 with an assasination that brought an Austrian threat upon Serbia, the mobilization of Russian forces for the protection of Serbia, and then a declaration of war by Germany to protect Austria. The war eventually brought the U.S. to mobilization, but none of this mattered to America's small farmers struggling to make a living and start a family.

World events especially didn't matter to Charles and Pearl. They were griefstricken by the death of their first born. Charles's reaction was to bury himself into the work of the farm. Perhaps he felt that if he could have a series of bumper crops, they would have enough money to somehow prevent any future such tragedies. Pearl was deeply distraught and felt that a black cloud of despair had fallen upon the family. However, she knew that she was pregnant and would soon have another chance with her second child. She had occasionally assisted Dr. Henry as a mid-nurse. She went to the doctor and asked for medical material to study. Over the next few months Pearl read everything she could about medicine and ailments. Then, on August 7, 1916, Pearl gave birth to Charles Ralph Gregory, Jr. Pearl rallied to this second chance and doted on Charles, Sr.'s namesake. She did everything in her power to protect him. She felt that sanitation was of primary importance, so Pearl cleaned everything and washed clothes often. She kept young Charles clean and protected from outside germs and bacteria. Most importantly, she boiled all water before using it.

Pearl and Charles continued to have more children who remained healthy. Another May daughter was born May 25, 1918. They named her Juanita Arline and called her Nita. Then the next year, on December 23, 1919, Pearl gave birth to another boy. He was named Donald Farold. He had dark auburn hair with an abundance of freckles, so he was eventually nick-named Speck, a name he was known by throughout the rest of his long life. Two years later, on December 29, 1921, Pearl gave birth to Chester Earl (Chet). Then Delbert Eugene (Del) was born June 10, 1923, and finally Melvin Eugene (Mel) was born on January 26, 1925. Del and Mel were named in honor of the late twin boys of Charles, Sr.'s brother Earl. Earl's twins, Del Eugene and Mel Eugene, like Neva and so many other infants of the era, had met an early death.

Pearl and Charles were extremely proud of their family — six happy, healthy, strong children, each one as intelligent and energetic as the next. Charles, Jr. was very strong and hard working. Nita was precocious and serious. Speck was a great talker, and people loved to listen to his stories. He was personable, intelligent, nimble, and tenacious. Chet, although intelligent, had an overactive sense of humor leaning toward obnoxiousness. He also was adept at finding ways to get out of work, and at pestering the younger boys. Delbert was the tallest of the children, dedicated to hard work, and he possessed an uncanny ability to retain facts and trivia. Mel, the youngest, was hardworking, short, adventuresome, strong, and free spirited. Everything was in place for happiness to abound for the family. But happiness depended on hard work in this distinctively different piece of land on the Columbia Plateau, between the Palouse Hills and the Channeled Scablands; this Texas Draw tract of Winona Country — one of the most geographically peculiar regions of the Northwest Inland Empire.

Chapter 3

This Peculiar Land of Winona

… And there is a time for every event under heaven… A time to plant, and a time to uproot what is planted… a time to tear down, and a time to build up…

—Ecclesiastes 3:1–3

The Winona country is part of a larger political area known as Whitman County. One of 39 counties in Washington State, it is a distinctively rich farming country and renowned as the most productive wheat-growing region in the world. Along with 15 other counties, Whitman is located in the geographical region known as the Columbia Plateau. And this so-called plateau is part of a larger economic and cultural region known as the Inland Empire, or the Inland Northwest.

The Inland Empire is made up of eastern Washington, northern Idaho (the panhandle), and western Montana. It is bordered by the Cascade Mountains to the west and the Rockies to the east. At 49 degrees, Canada lies to the north, and approximately 46 degrees north longitude provides most of the southern boundary.

The economic and cultural center of the empire is provided by the Spokane–Coeur d'Alene corridor. Other major cities include Yakima, Omak, Wenatchee, Pasco, Richland, Kennewick, Walla Walla, Moscow-Pullman, Lewiston-Clarkston, Missoula, and Butte. Major rivers include the Columbia, Snake, Clark Fork, Yakima, and Spokane. The region is bisected by I-90, the major transportation route. The Inland Empire has diverse resources, but it is primarily a producer of agricultural goods, minerals, and timber.

This region is politically and culturally diverse, but a plurality of the populous is fiscally and socially conservative, leaning toward small government and low taxes. The people are generally hard-working with a pioneer spirit of self-sufficiency. A large percentage are sportsmen with interest in bird hunting—primarily pheasants, grouse, partridge, quail, and chukar. There are also many deer and elk hunters. Due to the hunting enthusiasm and a rugged individualism, the vast majority of the people in this Inland Empire are pro-gun rights and supportive of the Second Amendment as a fundamental, guaranteed right.

Finally, some of the inhabitants of the region have had a history of separatism over the past century. Many in eastern Washington feel they are not represented in the state capital of Olympia. Although a larger land mass than western Washington, the eastern portion of the state has a much smaller population and therefore fewer representatives in the state legislature. Those in western Washington have a much more liberal political and cultural leaning and a larger population. Consequently, those in the east have little control over the events and laws of the state.

One tangential example of this is the vote to support higher taxes and user fees as well as state general budget funding for the Seattle Seahawks stadium. Of the 39 counties in the state, only King and Pierce had a majority vote for the funding of the stadium. In the remaining 37 counties, a majority voted against the state funding. However, the population of those two counties was so large that they carried the vote, much to the consternation of eastern Washington's residents.

Although Idaho is not as diverse, a similar situation occurs in the panhandle. The smaller population in the north is constantly overruled by the Boise crowd.

Whether real or perceived, the consequence of this lack of representation over the decades has resulted in a movement to form the state of Columbia. That is, eastern Washington, northern Idaho, and western Montana would break away from their states to form a somewhat homogenous state. Of course, this would be a near impossibility. The majority in each state would have to approve the separation, and for a variety of reasons that is extremely unlikely.

Nevertheless, for over 100 years there has been a movement to form the state of Columbia. Ironically, when Washington became a state, the proposed name was Columbia, but legislators felt that the state of Columbia would be confused with the District of Columbia. Today of course, D.C. is more commonly known as Washington, so the confusion exists in spite of the attempt to alleviate it back in 1889 when Washington achieved statehood.

Within this Inland Empire lies the Columbia Plateau, a geographical designation in Washington State. The region has been called a basin by some geographers, but it is actually a highland region bordered by mountains on each side and made up of rolling hills, plains, basins, ravines, gullies, draws, U-shaped valleys, mesas, hummocks, buttes, benches, channels, steptoes, and hillocks. It is not a true flat plateau, but that is probably the most accurate designation for the region.

The region is politically bordered by Idaho to the east and Oregon to the south; Pend Oreille, Stevens, Ferry, and Okanogan counties to the north; and Skagit, Snohomish, King, Pierce, Lewis, and Skamania counties to the west. The region is made up of 16 counties. Seven are named after native words, names, or tribes, including Chelan, Kittitas, Yakima, Klickitat, Spokane, Walla Walla, and Asotin. The other eight counties are named after presidents, political leaders, or explorers, including Lincoln, Adams, Grant, Garfield, Douglas, Benton, Franklin, Whitman, and Columbia (Columbus). Much of this region is sparsely populated, and the primary economic contributions are agricultural.

The Columbia Plateau is geographically bordered by the Cascades on the west, the Benewah and Bitterroot ranges on the east, the Blue Mountains on the south, and the Okanogan Highlands on the north. The Highlands are made up of a number of ridges, low lying mountain ranges, and trench river valleys that run primarily north to south. The V-shaped river valleys were carved out by glaciers during past ice ages. Towering above these trenches are the Selkirk, Chewelah, San Poil, and Huckleberry mountains, as well as the Kettle River Range.

Although there is diversity, the climate of the Columbia Plateau is considered dry with extremes of temperature. Most of the region has an annual precipitation of 10–20 inches, compared to western Washington, most of which receives 50–80 inches annually. Also, compared to western Washington, the plateau is colder in the winter, hotter in the summer, colder in the evening, and hotter during the day. This is known as a continental climate. That is, due to the prevailing winds (westerlies) and the Cascade Range, the region's climate is only marginally affected by the cooling Pacific Ocean.

The orographic effect plays a large role in the Pacific Northwest. The land heats up and cools down much more quickly than the ocean. Therefore the westerly winds act as an air conditioner and keep western Washington cooler in the summer and warmer in the winter. Land farther away from the ocean and separated by mountains tends to have more extreme temperatures. This also affects precipitation. As water evaporates off the ocean, it forms clouds. The westerlies blow those clouds toward the Coastal and then Cascade ranges, and that forces the clouds to rise and become cooler. Cooler air cannot retain as much water, so rain falls. As the remaining clouds descend eastward, down the slopes of the Cascades, the air becomes warmer at this lower elevation, and the air retains more water, resulting in little precipitation.

The west sides of these ranges are known as the windward sides, and the east sides are referred to as the leeward sides, or the rain shadows. The Columbia Plateau is in such a rain shadow.

Consequently, the area on the west side of the plateau receives only about 3–10 inches of annual precipitation, and that is considered arid or desert-like. As the westerlies carry those clouds farther east to the Palouse Hills in eastern Whitman County, the clouds begin to rise again and release some rainfall. Therefore most of the Palouse Hills have 12–18 inches of precipitation and are thus considered semi-arid. Winona is located between these two areas and receives approximately 8–10 inches per year. That is a big part of the marginality of Charles's farmland. Ten inches can produce a good crop, while 8 inches will possibly reach the breaking point—just enough to pay most of the debts and bills.

The other part of the marginality has to do with the soil. To understand the land itself, we must go back millions of years to the beginning of its formation. Most volcanos blow their tops and spew pulverized rock and lava. However, in this area it was different. Over millions of years, magma slowly rose to the surface of the plateau area, and the resulting lava slowly spread out in layers—perhaps several dozen layers—which hardened to form bedrock. The accumulated weight of these many heavy layers of hardened lava resulted in the lowering of this area below the surrounding land formations. However, some of the tops of granite mountains in the plateau still stand out as peaks. The most notable is Steptoe Butte. It is a relatively low, sharp peak referred to as a butte. Steptoe is so unusual that a few similar formations in Europe and Asia are referred to as steptoes. With the many layers of hard basalt bedrock laid down here, wind storms blew dust into the area primarily from the southwest. Wherever there was an outcrop, a dust shadow or accumulation formed. Over hundreds of thousands of years, these dust shadows built up to form hills that looked similar to sand dunes.

Additionally, the soil was built up by recurring layers of pulverized rock from eruptions of the Cascade volcanoes. Mount Mazama, Glacier Peak, Mount Hood, Mount Adams, Mount St. Helens, and Mount Rainier were such volcanos that erupted dozens of times in the past several hundred thousand years. They often sent plumes of pulverized rock thousands of feet upward into the atmosphere. With the westerlies blowing in the direction of the Columbia Plateau, many layers of powdery rock were mixed in with the dust-storm layers of this soil. The most recent example occurred on May 18, 1980, as Mt. St. Helens erupted. The resulting plume was carried around the world, but the fine powdery ash fell to earth in the Palouse Hills. This layer contributed additional nutrients to the silty loam soil and also helped prevent evaporation. Consequently, the following years resulted in bumper crops for Whitman County wheat farmers.

The combination of several hundred thousand years of these accumulations eventually formed the Palouse Hills, which stretched almost to the Columbia River and formed gently rolling hills of deep, nutrient-rich soils called *loess*. A similar type of soil occurs in Germany, and that is where the term *loess* originated. This Palouse Hills formation stretched much farther west prior to the ice ages, especially the last ice age. During the end of that ice age, estimated at 10,000–15,000 years ago, several floods stormed through this region and washed away soil between the areas of current-day Winona all the way south to the Snake River and west to the Columbia River. This was likely the world's greatest series of floods.

The earliest and greatest of these floods took place in just a few days, during which more water was carried through the region than flows in all of the earth's rivers today. This scoured away most of the loess in the area known as the Channeled Scablands. Much of this area is exposed bedrock basalt, but like little islands of loess, hummocks are left. Most of the hummocks have steep north sides where the gentle slope was abruptly washed away, but they also have gentle south slopes which are still adequate for farming. But where did those floods originate?

Approximately 15,000–18,000 years ago, the ice-age glaciers pushed south from Canada. At the site of current day Missoula, Montana, arms of the glaciers formed an ice dam to impound precipitation as well as the water that flowed from the Rockies, the Clark Fork River, and nearby drainages. Eventually a glacial lake was formed that reached an estimated 500 cubic miles.

Over the next 2,000 years, the earth warmed and the ice dam began to melt. As the dam melted, the lake grew higher and floated the ice dam. The result was an enormous flood that rushed across northern Idaho and into the Spokane Valley. This flood is sometimes referred to as the Spokane Flood. It took paths westward, west by southwest, and the southwest tract, which created the Cheney-Palouse Scablands. That tract came through the Winona area to the Palouse River, then to the Snake River, the Columbia, and on to the Pacific. The water was so high that it backed up river valleys so that they flowed upstream.

Erratic rocks, those out of place from far away, were left throughout the flooded areas. The erratic rocks were carried by unmelted pieces of the glacier. The bedrock was scoured clean in many areas. The Glacial Lake Missoula would then fill again, but at a lower level, and then flood again. It is estimated that as many as 36 of these floods took place at approximately 50-year intervals. Each time more soil was scoured away from these channeled scablands.

This Cheney-Palouse tract took that path because the land sloped down from the northeast to the southwest. Due to fissures in the bedrock, several lakes were created. These lakes in the region all run from northeast to southwest. One of the grandest of these is Rock Lake, several hundred feet deep, measuring 9 miles from northeast to southwest, and surrounded on three sides with steep, columnar basalt cliffs.

Rock Lake also has an interesting if not chilling history, coupled with myth. First, due to the depth of the lake and the high cliffs, the water is colder than most lakes in the region. Second, due to the long, narrow formation of the lake, it is quite windy, and some locals refer to it as "the wind tunnel." Finally, just under the surface in some areas, the cliffs descending underwater turn into caves that curve back dozens of feet in depth. Consequently, there have been several capsized boats, a canoe, and, most recently, a kayak in the lake; and in almost each instance the bodies of the sportsmen were not recovered.

Also, at one time in the early 1900s, a train derailed and some of the cars fell into the lake, never to be recovered. A myth continues that sometimes at night you can hear the eerie wail of the train's melancholy whistle. Another myth persists about the tortured soul of a Native American chief who wanders the area near Rock Lake and along the banks of the Palouse River near Winona. Chief Kamiakin, a son of the local Palouse Chief Kamiak, traveled far and wide as a free spirit in his youth. He had met Commusni, a daughter of the Yakama Chief Weowicht. Kamiakin married her and became a leader of both tribes and a respected hunter and warrior throughout the Columbia Plateau. He was wounded in the fight with Colonel Steptoe at the Battle of Rosalia. He then retired to live a quiet life in the vicinity of Rock Lake and the Palouse River, near his father's resting place.

When he died, Kamiakin was buried near his beloved Rock Lake. However, a museum owner from back East dug up the body and removed the skeletal remains of the head and shoulders. Kamiakin's upset progeny then took the remnants of his remains and reburied them at a secret location south of the lake, possibly near Winona. People still say they have seen a glimpse of a dark figure in the distance around the area. Then before they get too close, the figure vanishes.

Many areas of the channeled scablands formed lakes or potholes or were simply washed away to the bedrock. But hummocks like those on the Gregory homestead were left above the main flooded area of the tract. However, as the water backed up, it scoured the northern and inside edges to make them steep, and it created a flood plain between them. The west branch of Texas Draw on the north border of the homestead was washed clean of soil down to the bedrock of basalt. Nevertheless land on the south slopes of the hummocks was still suitable for farming, but only with very hard work and the right precipitation. That's what Charles, Sr. had to work with as a farm. It was difficult work, but he was happy for the opportunity.

Palouse Falls, 200 feet high, breaks into the
plunge pool formed from glacial age floods.
The Palouse River then meanders south
for 6 miles as it gently empties
into the Snake River.

Aunt Elsie
spent time
w/cousin
Delbert

Beside his great-grandson Trenton Eugene,
Delbert Eugene Gregory stands, in 2012,
before the homestead where he was born
almost 90 years earlier. Note the homestead's west hummock base to the right.

Chapter 4

More Joys and Sorrows
1915–1928

Oh heart, if one should say to you that the soul perishes like the body, answer that the flower withers, but the seed remains.

—Kahlil Gibran

In 1915, Charles, Sr. joined a semi-pro baseball team—very semi! They tuned up their skills by playing local town teams from Pine City, St. John, Lacrosse, Colfax, and Endicott. On the weekends they traveled to Spokane and played at least three games. The players in this league were paid, but only on their performance. They received two-bits for a hit and a dollar for a homerun. This doesn't seem like much money, but in the early 1900s most laborers received only one or two dollars for a hard day's work. Besides, Charles was having some fun and a well-deserved break from the toil on the farm. He was the catcher for the Winona Wildcats and teamed up with some outstanding ball players. The center fielder for the team was Elmer Leifer. Elmer was noted for having one of the highest batting averages in the league. He went on to play professional ball for an Arkansas minor league team. However, the talented young man lost an eye in a collision, and his baseball career ended. Leifer had many progeny that were outstanding St. John High School athletes, several of whom were noted state "B" basketball players. Another heavy hitter for the Wildcats was Claude James. There were three James brothers on that team, all very talented, but Claude was known for his powerful and prolific hitting. He often made upwards of $5 a day from his hitting skills. The fans in Spokane referred to him as Clobberin' Claude, and most swore that he was better than Babe Ruth, since Claude averaged a pair of homeruns per game and seldom struck out. Claude was offered a contract for the Boston Braves, but he refused to travel away from his family. Charles enjoyed playing baseball, but when Neva passed away in 1916 he never played again. After that he threw himself into the farm work, and that was his life from then on.

As the Gregory children were born and started growing up on the homestead, they found much to do in work and play. Young Charles, Jr. was able to follow his dad and granddad around the farm and watch, learn, and help. He learned to milk cows, feed livestock, and clean barns, and he also learned the important task of swathing the grain. By the time he was six, Charles, Jr. could take a hand-held, sharp, metal sickle to the back slope to cut the wheat stocks and then bundle them in the field. He then helped to gather up these bundled shocks of wheat and place them in the wagon. Charles, Jr. also rode Caesar to and from the fields. However, when work was done, he rode the pony for the joy of freedom. Young Charles rode to Rock Creek to fish for trout, to Texas Lake to pull some catfish, or to Green Lake. The so-called lake was just a Rock Creek plunge pool formed by Towell Falls, which rose 15 feet above the creek and fell over columnar basalt cliffs. In spring the falls were quite substantial and created a large pool abundant with life, including crayfish or crawdads, periwinkles, stone fly and caddis fly larvae, shiners, minnows, sculpins, frogs, and various water bugs. All these life forms created an abundance of food for the large, numerous carp that lived or were at least flushed into the lake from upstream.

As Nita grew she learned to ride Jenny, a small female mule. She helped her mother shred cabbage and convert it into sauerkraut. Nita always helped her mother with cooking, cleaning, tending the garden, and separating cream from the milk. This last duty was usually performed by Grandfather William, but since it was done twice daily, everyone helped out at one time or another. The freshly drawn milk was poured into a large metal bowl, and the separating machine was hand-cranked for several minutes. A cream can was placed under the spout as it was slid into place. The spout pushed open a hole, and the cream immediately exited via the spout and the can was filled. Then the milk was drained off into a large can. Most of the milk was sold in Winona, and the cream was kept for pouring over oatmeal and making butter. Nita made butter by hand-shaking a jar until the cream turned to butter. She also helped with baking pies in the wood stove, and canning fruits, vegetables, jellies, and jams. Her mother was quite frugal when it came to using the available ingredients. One of the family's favorite jellies was actually made from corn cobs. After the ears of corn had been boiled and the kernels sliced off for canning, there were always remnants of corn left on the cob. Pearl and Nita boiled the cobs and reduced the liquid. Pectin and sugar were added to the mixture, and the result was a delicious, light-pink tinted, transparent jelly.

Another favorite that led to some playful joking was Pearl's buckshot pie. Wild elderberry bushes grew along much of Rock Creek and Texas Lake. The berries grew in bunches and were available throughout most of the year except deep winter. When Pearl didn't have her own gooseberries or raspberries, she prompted the boys to pick the wild elderberries for her pies. These berries had hard seeds that slightly softened up when cooked. Nevertheless, there were always a few hard seeds in every pie. The boys loved their mother and sister's elderberry pies but learned to eat them very carefully. Consequently, the term *buckshot pie* was an inside joke the boys laughed about for decades to come.

Headcheese was an additional popular food on the homestead. After putting it down, gutting, boiling, and scraping the hair from a butchered hog, the head was taken to Pearl. She burned off any remaining fine hairs, further boiled the head, and sliced off a few slabs of meat from the jowls. This would be used for sandwiches or sliced into a potato or sauerkraut dish. Then she took the remaining head to the cool cellar and placed it in a covered crock pot. Each day she sliced off pieces from the head, including snout, jowl, ear, tongue, cartilage, fat, and meat. This was added to boiling water and well salted. The rendered mixture was poured into a pan and placed in the ice box. The next morning she had a congealed slab of headcheese. Neither the process nor the finished product sound appetizing, but the boys said headcheese was one of the finest tasting foods they had ever eaten.

As Speck, Chet, and Delbert grew, they too had chores along with fun on the farm. Delbert recalled, "When I was about 3 years of age, I rode to Green Lake with Granddad and my older brothers in the wagon. We took along pitchforks to spear the large carp." He continued, "Some of the carp were a yard long and weighed over fifty pounds. Some were so heavy and active that they flopped on the fork with enough momentum to jostle us into the shallow lake." Spending the better part of a day at this large pool, they filled the wagon with carp and took it back to the farm, where the bronze colored fish were chopped up and fed to the pigs. A few of the bony carp were kept for the dinner table, but even with the best preparation and removal of the muddy tasting blood-line, they were not very appetizing. Once, when they unloaded and butchered the carp, one was still alive, active, and apparently healthy enough to survive. Delbert put the fish in the front wooden watering trough and it remained healthy and alive throughout the spring, summer, and autumn. That was the first of little Delbert's wild pets. Over time, Delbert adopted many more such wild animals, and they provided him with some of his best childhood memories.

There was one enjoyable and profitable task that the children performed each year during the birthing of the lambs: They got to raise the orphaned lambs. The Leonard Henderson family lived about 4 miles farther north on Texas Draw. The Henderson Sheep Ranch was about a mile south of Revere. They had a vast herd of sheep, and each spring several dozen ewes gave birth. Usually about a half dozen ewes had problem pregnancies. They suffered from prolapsed uterus during delivery. The condition, prevalent among sheep, usually resulted in healthy lambs but always resulted in the death of the ewe. Each of the Gregory children was responsible for one lamb. They got milk from their cows and bottle-fed the lambs. After the lambs were several weeks old, the Gregory kids sold the lambs back to Len Henderson. It was a profitable experience for both the kids and the sheep rancher. The lambs would have otherwise died, and the kids got the double benefit of a temporary pet and some pocket change.

The kids had a good time on the farm; it provided freedom. The kids freely roamed the wide open spaces of the countryside. They saw all assortments of wild animals—whitetail deer, mule deer, badgers, coyotes, raccoons, skunks, porcupines, rattlesnakes, bobcats, and cougars. Once they even saw a black panther (melanistic cougar). They also noted an abundance of pheasants, partridge, quail, and the native lesser prairie chicken. By age ten, Charles, Jr. was using the Browning 12-gauge to bring the occasional wild game bird to the table. The children rode the two horses and the smaller mules around the central plain of the farm, up on the mesas, through the barren draw, and to each body of water they could find. They explored basalt caves and scaled all manner of rock structures.

They enjoyed life, and Charles, Sr. and Pearl were happy for their children. The loss of Neva seemed as if a nightmare of long ago. Charles, Jr. was responsible and hard-working, but always with a playful spirit. Nita was extremely intelligent and learned quickly from her mother. She could read at 4 years of age and remained an outstanding student as the children went to the Turner School. The school was a 2-mile ride and, remarkably, the children had almost perfect attendance. Charles, Jr. let Nita and Speck ride Caesar, and Chet and he rode the work horse. Delbert and Mel were too young for school at this time, but the last day of school in 1928 arrived with an adventure for little Delbert. He would be eligible to start school the following autumn, and children of his age were invited to attend the last day of school. Delbert got to ride on the back of the work horse behind Charles, Jr. and Chet. He doesn't remember too much about the day, but he does recall a large picnic with plenty of good food and lots of games to play. He remembers just watching everyone else laughing and having fun. He was looking forward to attending Turner School the following September.

Charles, Jr.'s 6th Grade report card was signed by his teacher Miss Eva Stephens for the year that began September 6, 1927, and ended May 17, 1928. The report further stated that L. T. Babcock was the County Superintendent and that Charles, Jr. attended 173 days with no absences on days that school was in session. His health habits were listed as excellent, and deportment was 96%. Percentages were used in lieu of letter grades. All of Charles's grades were equivalent to A's, between 92% and 100%. His highest grades were in arithmetic and spelling, each at 100%.

Turner School District Number 195 was a member of the Whitman County Public School System. It was established in 1906 in Mrs. Turner's log cabin, but a new building was erected about 2 miles north of Texas Lake in 1910. The lumber was purchased on credit from the Potlatch Lumber Company. They were never paid in full, so Potlatch took the district to court. The school district won the case and the court stated that a public school could not be compelled to pay if the funds would take learning materials away from students. They further cited the 1889 state constitution. The organic document states that education is the paramount duty of the state and not to be abridged for other concerns. In 1920 the Revere School District consolidated with Turner; in 1932 Turner consolidated with Winona; in 1955 Winona consolidated with the Endicott School District; and in 1987 Endicott and St. John formed a high school combination and an elementary school cooperative.

When Charles, Jr. and Speck were ages 12 and 9, respectively, they rode the horses north to Rock Lake for fishing and overnight camping. That was a great time for them, and in later years, Speck often talked about those early days of fishing. They first stopped at Ewan to stay overnight with Uncle Earl and Aunt Stella. Then, after serving them a big breakfast, Stella sent them on their way with bread, fruit, and cookies for their journey north to the lake. The boys' uncle gave them some freshly dug night crawlers. They carried a tobacco tin from their pipe-smoking grandfather, and in it were hooks that were specially prepared for use if they ran out of live bait. They had learned how to prepare the hooks from Bill Aldrich, the adult son of a neighboring farmer. Bill often hired-out to help with the Gregory homestead after his work was done on his father's farm. One day he took the boys to the chicken coop and showed them how to gently remove a couple of long narrow feathers from the rooster's neck. He tied a feather to the back of the hook bend and then tightly wound it forward in close circles and tied it down on the front. The hackle of the feather fanned out, making the fishing hook appear like a caterpillar or some other fuzzy bug. Sometimes he started the preparation by tying in a piece of red wool yarn at the bend of the hook. Other times they took an eye feather from the peacock and tied this in before attaching some of the rooster hackle. Bill told the boys they could use these specially prepared hooks to trick the fish.

Charles, Jr. discovered that these hooks worked as well as live bait, especially near the southern outlet of Rock Lake. He fished with a 5-foot stick, tied about 5 feet of thin, heavy rope to the end, and then added about three feet of thin, strong, doubled strand of twine fibers for leader. He then tied the prepared hook to the twine strand and flung it upstream into the ripples. The line then swung down over the ripples into a small pool. After about a half-dozen of these casts, he usually picked up a strike, jerked back to set the hook, and lifted a large German brown trout from the creek. They also fished in the lake using earthworms as bait and were equally blessed with a bounty of fish. In the evening they built a campfire, spread their bedrolls, and sat on a log while they roasted fresh fish over the fire. In later life Speck often shared that those were some of his best moments.

A few times they went farther north to Sprague and visited the Pless family (their Uncle Earl's in-laws). Charles got to know some of the neighboring kids and became fast friends with Ernest Harold Loy, another young boy who shared an interest in fishing. Ernie took Charles and Speck to his secret fishing hole, a wide spot about 30 yards upstream from the Sprague Lake inlet. They caught cut-throat trout that had broad shoulders and deep orange meat. The boys camped out and roasted those fish over an open fire. Building on these early years, Ernie remained a close friend to Charles, Jr. throughout his life and to Charlie's dying day, many years later aboard the *Hokusen Maru*.

One incident that was scary for Charles, Jr., and probably more frightening for his Grandpa William, involved a rattlesnake. When William accompanied his grandson on one of his first pheasant hunts, William had stopped to instruct Charles, Jr. on the proper positions to hold the Browning 12-guage and then proper behavior in the field during hunting. As William stood there next to the sagebrush, he heard a familiar sound of a rattler. It sounded close, very close. In fact, the snake was coiled up between William's legs — coiled and ready to strike. The old man quietly told his grandson to shoot it and then held his breath. Without hesitation, Charles lowered the gun and fired at the ground beneath William. The snake was separated from its head. William was relieved, and Charles, Jr. had bagged his first diamondback rattler. William plucked out his pocket knife, cut off the rattles, and handed Charles, Jr. his first hunting souvenir.

At about this time, Pearl noticed that each morning she had one less chicken in the coop. Feathers were strewn throughout the pen and a hole dug under the wire. Each time she filled the hole in with rocks, only to find another hole the following day. She was happy one morning when she discovered no lost chickens, but as she was on the front porch snapping string beans, she heard a commotion from the coop. Pearl grabbed the .22 rifle, ran to the pen, and saw a coyote chasing the hens. She raised the firearm and fired. The coyote fell, and she dragged it to the porch for Charles, Sr. to skin later in the day. Pearl checked on baby Mel in the bassinette on the porch and returned to her task preparing the beans. After about an hour, the coyote stood, shook its head, growled, and snapped as it charged baby Mel. Pearl quickly picked up a piece of firewood and beat-in the coyote's skull. Apparently she had simply grazed the wild canine's head when she shot—only enough to temporarily knock it out. Just another day on the farm!

This family survived the hardships and prospered, and the boys often regaled one another with their childhood adventures. They confided that they had never seen their father so happy as the time he purchased a new piece of equipment for the farm—it was a riding plow. Now he could sit while tilling the soil. It was much better than being harnessed up and trudging through the plowed ground. Also, this made it easier for William, now in his sixties. Charles, Sr. was proud of his accomplishments by 1926. It had been difficult, but by the time he was 34, his farm was productive and he had a hard working, spirited, loving wife; an intelligent, hardworking daughter; and five active sons, each as strong and smart as the next. However, 1926 was to be a devastating year for the family and the beginning of the end of farming for this industrious but unfortunate family.

In early March, Charles came down with a hard case of a particularly virulent influenza. Numerous people in the region had come down with that flu, and it was deadly for many. Charles was sick, dizzy, and dehydrated, and he had trouble standing, walking, and breathing for several days. One morning the need to keep the farm work moving along overpowered the insidious illness. Charles, Sr. pulled himself out of bed and he returned to work long hours on the farm. It's what he had to do to keep the farm going. He felt it was necessary. However, after a long day of this work he returned to bed, almost unable to breathe. He passed out and fell into a deep sleep and passed into the hands of the Lord late that evening. The Spokane newspaper, the *Spokesman Review* printed the following obituary:

WINONA YOUNG MAN DEAD.

Leaves Wife and Six Children—Is victim of Pneumonia.

Influenza and pneumonia caused the death of Charles Ralph Gregory, Sr. of the Winona country, last Saturday night. He was the

second man from Winona to succumb to the dread disease within a
week, W. D. Muir having died on the previous Saturday.

Mr. Gregory, who was only 34 years of age, is survived by his
wife and six children, Charles, Jr., Juanita, Donald, Chester, Delbert,
and Melvin. One brother, Guy Gregory, lives at Lind, and a brother,
Earl Gregory, lives at Ewan. Mr. Gregory had been a resident of
Whitman county since 1910, having come here from Kansas.

Funeral services were held in the Winona cemetery Wednesday
afternoon.

The obituary in the *Colfax Gazette* (currently named *Whitman
County Gazette*) follows:

*Charles Ralph Gregory, Sr., aged 34 years, passed over the great
divide from his home at Texas Lake, about 10 o'clock last Saturday
evening. Mr. Gregory had been ill with the flu a few days, had
apparently recovered, and was at his farm work, when suddenly he
was taken down with pneumonia, and the end came soon. Mr.
Gregory came here from Kansas in 1910, and was well known as a
man of sterling character and untiring industry. He is survived by
his wife, Mrs. Pearl Gregory, six children, his father W. T. Gregory,
two brothers, Earl and Guy, a sister Mrs. E. Menzie of Copeland,
Kansas, who came to attend the funeral. Internment was made at the
Winona cemetery on Wednesday afternoon, March 10.*

His funeral was officiated by Reverend S. E. Hormbrook, who
read scripture from *Revelations* as well as the following poem:

> *How sweet to sleep where all is peace,*
> *Where sorrow cannot reach the breast,*
> *Where all life's idle throbbings cease*
> *And pain is lulled to rest!*

Song selections by the Winona Baptist Church Choir included
Beautiful Isle of Somewhere and *Nearer My God to Thee*. Floral offerings
were made by Mr. and Mrs. C. V. Kuehl, Mr. and Mrs. Harry Kiehle,
Merle Habbick, The Texas Draw Community Club, Mr. and Mrs.

F. T. Maxwell, and Mr. and Mrs. Charles Brown. Ceremony and internment was provided by L. L. Bruning, Colfax, Washington.

The Texas Draw Community Club was especially supportive for Pearl at this time. Pearl had been a member of the club for over a decade by 1926. Previously she had been a major source of support for the other women, especially when they had children. Pearl was always there to deliver the babies, and she stayed on to help the mothers for a while after each delivery as the women set up schedules to assist each other. However, now, for the first time, she found herself dependent on assistance from the other club members.

Texas Draw was an area that stretched from about 3 miles northwest of Winona, with various branches north to about a mile south of Revere and a few miles south of Ewan. Along the draw and neighboring branches resided about a dozen farm families. They were somewhat isolated, so around 1914 many of the farm wives decided to form the group. We think of women's support groups as being something fairly new and a modern invention. However, that is exactly what they formed a century ago—a women's support group. Besides Pearl Gregory and her closest friend, Edith Brown, two women who lost their husbands in 1926 and 1927, respectively, there were about a dozen other farm wives in the support group. Some of those included the wives of the farm families of Maxwell, Gailey, McCucheon, Jordan, Gallaher, Lamb, Conover, Henderson, and Sharp. These were strong women who had a valiant pioneer spirit. They were resolute and resourceful. This was a tough, dry, windy, dusty area in which their husbands had to work long hours in order to raise a crop. The wives had to be equally hard-working, strong willed, and supportive of their husbands. These women had long work days and continuous tasks to perform. They all milked cows, fed livestock, and tended large gardens—gardens that were necessary for sustenance, not just hobby gardens. The farm women were responsible for the cleanliness and organization of their households and their children. Almost all of these women had children at somewhat regular intervals—usually each bore a child every 18 to 24 months. The women kept track of each other's pregnancies and arranged a schedule to help those most in need of assistance. Of course, Pearl gained a lot of experience as a mid-nurse, and she proved to be an essential member of the club. But with the death of Charles, Sr., her world drastically changed; and now she was in dire need of the active club and its supportive members.

The death was at least temporarily debilitating to Pearl, and it was a shocking and confusing time for her fatherless children. For William it was also a devastating blow. In 1910, at the age of 46, he had traveled to this dry, marginal region to help his hard-working son start a farm. Now, at the age of 63, he was responsible for a farm, a daughter-in-law, and six grandchildren. One can only wonder what he was experiencing. Surely he realized that he couldn't do the work of Charles. Many in the local community swore that Charles, Sr. accomplished more in one day than any two men. The future looked bleak for William without his son. But more dark clouds loomed on the horizon—figuratively and literally.

When William was riding the work horse along the back boundaries of the property one morning, he heard the rattle of a western diamondback rattlesnake. Suddenly the horse spooked and threw William headfirst into a large patch of sagebrush, where a hard, dead branch penetrated his right eye. Badly bloodied and in horrendous pain, William remounted the horse and made it back to the house. Pearl helped to clean the wound, but the old man lost his eye and packed the socket with cotton. He eventually got a glass eye to place in the socket. The loss of the eye was a painful experience, but worse yet, his already poor eyesight was now questionable. Coupled with the early death of Charles, Sr., the emotional pain of William's disability left him a distraught and bitter man.

Nita was suffering from fevers and extremely painful, sore throats that early spring. Pearl took her to Dr. Henry in Endicott, and he sent her to Colfax for surgery. Nita had her tonsils removed. However, in the process of anesthetizing her, ether was accidentally squirted into her right eye. The anesthetic burned her cornea and inner eyelid, and the damage affected her eyesight. She was doubly pained by the removal of the tonsils and the severe burn to her eye. For several years after that, Nita had to wear glasses to correct the sight in her eye. Although less serious than the loss of William's eye, it was nevertheless a traumatic experience for the 8-year-old girl.

Wash day usually came once a week, when Pearl had Echo Maxwell, a young neighbor lady, help her. They filled a large, oblong, copper boiler with water, lifted it to the stovetop, and built a roaring fire. After the water had boiled for a sufficient time they lowered the boiler to the floor and placed clothes in it to soak. One laundry day before little Delbert's fourth birthday, he was trying to get out of someone's way as he stumbled and fell backwards into the copper boiler. His mother pulled him out in an instant and ripped off his clothes. He had burned his back, buttocks, and upper legs. With good medical care by his mother, eventually those burns healed without scars, except for his right thigh. The act of pulling the clothes off seemed like the correct thing to do. That way he could quickly cool-down. However, in the process of taking off his pants, the skin came off his right thigh. It took a great deal of doctoring and months to heal, but throughout the rest of his long life, Delbert always had a large, thick pad of white scar tissue covering the front of that thigh.

In the Winona country and the western part of the Columbia Plateau, the weather had been unpredictable during that previous year. The winter was extremely cold, but with very little snow. The spring was warmer and windier than usual. By the middle of June, it was extremely hot, with small tornados called dust devils, heavy dust storms, and dry thunderstorms. Although the dust devils were a common annual event, the tornados were much stronger that summer. One particularly strong tornado came through the area surrounding the homestead. It lifted several shingles off the house, barn, and outbuildings. However, it came through the area centered on the machine shed, and the entire roof was lifted off the shed. The next morning the boys discovered the roof deposited over three hundred yards away, down on the far side of the channeled scabland gulley of the west branch of Texas Draw.

The evening skies were lit up that June and July. They provided a show of booming thunder and bright lightning, but no rain. One evening in early July, lightning struck a little over a mile south of the homestead and ignited a fire that swept up over 1,000 acres, including all the family's wheat crop. After several weeks the crop insurance company sent an adjuster to the farm.

The short, portly man showed up in his dusty, black Model-A Ford one warm morning. William drove him back to the charred wheat field in the wagon accompanied by a couple of the boys. He had a long talk with William and the boys saw him throw his hat on the ground, pace off a distance and count the number of burned remnants of the wheat stalks. They rode back to the house and the adjuster pulled out a book, wrote, and then handed William a check. He was talking about the problems of the company and the large number of recent claims due to an act of God. William looked long at the check and dropped it to the ground. He had all he could take. The stress must have been overwhelming, for William pulled out his pocket knife, stuck it under the man's chin, and told him to get the hell off his land. The insurance agent hesitated as if paralyzed. His face turned bright red as droplets of sweat rolled down his nose and cheeks. He finally turned, ran to his new car as fast as his short legs would carry him, and sped off in a cloud of dust. Speck went over to the check and saw that it was written for $120. That was supposed to replace a crop that would have grossed a minimum of $3,000, if not $5,000.

A few days later in the early morning, William, Charles, Jr., and Speck walked to the barn for milking. William called out "Bossy, Baawww-ssseeee, Bosseee!" Bossy quickly moved to the barn, swaying side to side but going as fast as she could waddle. She was trailed by Jersie and Guernsie. The old man took out a cream can, scooped up some chopped grain, threw it into the feed manger, added alfalfa, and stanchioned the cows' necks in place. After they milked the cows, William and the two eldest boys walked back toward the cellar to separate the rich liquid. Suddenly, William collapsed and fell to the dry ground! The boys called out for their mother. William's pail slammed to the ground, and the milk spilled out into a white pool. Just as suddenly, the thirsty ground absorbed the liquid. The milk was taken by this ground, just as William's hopes, dreams, and his very life were absorbed by this dry, barren land. William never gained consciousness. He passed away from a heart attack. He had lived to the age of 63 years and 6 months, a long life for someone born during the Civil War. The article in the *Colfax Gazette* stated:

> *Funeral services were held in Winona, on Tuesday, October 2, the Rev. G. M. Harrington being present to bury his old friend. As a community we mourn the loss of Mr. Gregory, as he was well and favorably known to us. And the sympathy of our people is extended to the survivors.*

Shocked, but stoic, Pearl realized that the responsibility of the farm lay upon her broad shoulders. She had a 320-acre farm, a home, and six children to care for, but she trudged on, never complaining. Her heart must have been broken by the circumstances she had experienced, especially during the past 7 months. But with her strong pioneer spirit, Pearl went on to work diligently for her children's futures. She continued to work the farm with the help of Charles, Jr. and Speck, who accomplished almost as much as most men. She had Chet, who shirked most manual labor, but she did have Nita as a great support to keep the household in shape. Delbert and Mel were just too young to contribute much. Delbert was 2 years of age when his father died and had just turned 3 prior to the death of his grandfather. Mel was only a year old during those tragedies. However, Pearl also had the help of several neighbors, such as Mr. and Mrs. Charles Brown and the young Bill Aldrich. The members of the Texas Draw Community Club and the Winona Baptist Church also helped with cooking and moral support. The early Twentieth Century support group of the Texas Draw Community Club provided valuable assistance to Pearl in 1926 and then to her friend Edith Brown the following year when Edith lost her husband, Charles Brown. Both women had contributed greatly over the previous dozen years, and now that benefit had come back to buoy their spirits and offer relief for their families.

Charles, Jr. had to grow up fast. All the kids had to grow up fast, but at age 10, Charles, Jr. was now the man of the house. He had to leave his childhood behind him. Like the rest of the kids, he still tried to have fun and explore, ride, and fish. Except for Delbert and Melvin, the kids still went to school every day that it was in session. They still completed their studies with high marks. But Charles, Jr. had to be much more responsible than before—more of an adult, but a playful adult who would always long for the freedom of his early childhood. In later years, in a Japanese prison camp during the worst of bouts with malaria, his close friend Ernie Loy said his buddy Charlie would call out for Caesar. In his foggy, malarial hallucinations at Cabanatuan Camp #1 on Luzon, 1943, Charles, Jr. was transported in time and space—riding the sagebrush hummocks and scabrock gullies of Texas Draw, back to Winona atop his trusty mount, Caesar.

Unfortunately, in 1928 no group of people could accomplish the efforts of Charles, Sr. Without the crop that previous year and negligible settlement from the insurance company, Pearl had to mortgage the farm. Their first mortgage over a dozen years earlier had been for lumber, livestock, equipment, tools, and farm implements. This mortgage was for the bare necessities of survival. After 2 years of attempting to keep the farm going, barely a tenth of the usual acres had been tilled, planted, and harvested. Pearl came to realize that the farm would not survive. The Winona Bank agreed with her: It foreclosed on the mortgage and took the farm, house, livestock, and machinery. Pearl was destitute.

Penniless but unshaken, Pearl found an opening for a mid-nurse in the Oakesdale doctors' office, working for Dr. Dolson Palmer and Dr. George Hurst. Pearl had a good deal of experience in this field, so she applied and was immediately hired. The bank sold and foreclosed the farm to several people before it eventually went to Bill and Nina Lamb and their sons Willis and Wilbur.

The farm is still in that family's hands under the supervision of Willis's son Marvin.

The Gregorys moved to a modest house in Oakesdale, and Pearl set about to create a new home for her children, as she worked hard and saved for the future. Her goal was to someday own and manage a restaurant. Her long-term goal was to put her children through college. Unknown to her, the stock market crash, a dozen years of national economic depression, and a world power struggle were about to take place. All these obstacles stood between her and the fulfillment of her dreams.

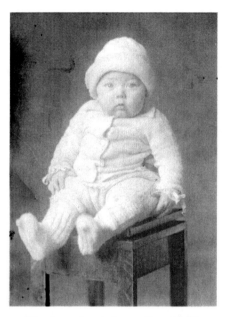

Charles, Jr. at 4 months, 1916.

Pearl and Charles, Jr., 1917.

Pearl and Charles, Jr.
at garden, 1923.

Charles, Jr. and Charles, Sr. with straw-powered
steam engine for the thresher, 1919.

Charles, Jr. and baby Chester with Papa L. C. Johnson's
Packard Touring Car, 1922.

Texas Draw Community Club, Nita, age 6, at front, right of center
with dark hair. Club members, L–R: Edith Brown, Mrs. Len
Henderson, Nina Lamb, Mrs. Sharp, Mrs. F. T. Maxwell
Mrs. Conover, Margaret Gallaher, and Pearl Gregory
holding baby Delbert, 1923.

Wheat harvest at the homestead: William Thomas, age 61, on
wagon; Charles Ralph Gregory, Jr., age 8, behind him, on
Caesar; and Charles Ralph Gregory, Sr., age 32, standing
in front of stationary thresher, 1924.

Charles, Jr., age 9, 1925.

Charles, Sr. with draft
mules, 1915.

Charles, Sr. with Nita, age 3,
on Jenny, 1921.

Baby Nita, Pearl, and
Charles, Jr., 1918.

Nita and Charles, Jr., 1918.

Speck on homestead porch, 1920. Note Maytag washing machine.

Speck and Nita, 1922. Note homemade jumpsuits.

Charles, Sr. with the horses, 1915.

Charles, Sr. with Browning 12-gauge, 1922.

Winona semi-pro baseball team, 1915. Front L–R: Claude James, G. James, H. James, Charles Gregory, Sr., C. V. Kuehl. Middle: J. Block, F. Ayler, J. Schroeder. Back: Bud Wagner, Elmer Leifer, Coach Mitch Taylor.

Pearl at the homestead, 1924.

William Gregory at
Homestead, 1926.

Bill Aldrich and Charles, Jr.,
1926.

Gregory children and neighbors at Winona homestead, 1927.
Front L–R: Chet, Delbert, Mel, Speck. Middle: Nadine Brown,
Nita, Eileen Brown. Back: Mr. Bill Brown and Charles, Jr.

Chapter 5

The Move to Oakesdale

Childhood is when the world to come is an adventure to be met...

—Len Webster

While Winona and Revere were both small, dwindling communities, Oakesdale, in the heart of the world's richest wheat farming country, was large and expanding. It was founded in 1888, the year prior to Washington statehood. Located in a depression between Steptoe Butte and Rosalia, the area was known as McCoy Valley, named after early settlers. The valley lies east of Tennessee Flats, Cashup Flats, and Naff Ridge, and north of the ridge to Rosalia. The McCoy family had fled Kentucky in 1875 to escape some of the turmoil and violence experienced between the post-Civil War factions in that region. The McCoy family members were among the first settlers in the valley. The town site of Oakesdale was platted in 1887 and named after Thomas Oakes, a vice-president of Northern Pacific Railroad. By the time the Gregorys arrived in Oakesdale in 1928, the community had two doctors (Palmer and Hurst), a flour mill (owned and operated by Joseph Barron, who developed the Nutri-Grain brand that he sold to Kellogg's), several grain elevators and warehouses, numerous stores (including three groceries— Piggly Wiggly, IGA, and Ripley's), two butcher shops, a bakery, two hotels (Southard's and Van Alstine's), two banks, and two blacksmith foundries (operated by Jack Dyer and by Bill Elkins, Sr.). The community also offered a photo shop (Klepfer's Studios), a print shop, a paint outlet, a second-hand store, a telephone operating center, a harness and buggy shop, three barbers, two hardware and implement outlets, a large variety store (Walker's), two general stores, three restaurants, three drug stores, one livery stable, five gas stations, a shoe shop, a furniture store, one movie theater, one trucking company, one dentist, two realtors, and three train depots with telegraphs. The train depots were operated by Northern Pacific, Great Northern, and the Oregon Washington Railroad & Navigation Company, the last of which became part of Union Pacific in 1939.

The town also had Oakesdale School District Number 69 for 1st through 12th graders, and there were nine surrounding country schools for 1st through 8th graders. Those included Harlan, Upper Thorn Creek, Lower Thorn Creek, Granite Hill, Pleasant Hill, Deep Cut, Crabtree, Fairbanks, and the Fletcher School. Oakesdale eventually absorbed the country grade schools by 1938, the northern half of the Belmont School District in 1943, and the Farmington School District in 1969. Thereafter the district was officially designated Oakesdale Consolidated School District Number 324.

Additionally, the town had half a dozen saloons with a wild reputation for Saturday night fights, including knifings and an occasional shooting incident. However, to counterbalance the rough and tumble bar scene, Oakesdale also provided church services from seven different denominations, including Northern Methodist, Southern Methodist, Baptist, Presbyterian, Catholic, the Church of Christ, and the Grace Union Church.

When the Gregorys arrived in Oakesdale, the family matriarch was busy establishing her own household, but she did a great deal for other households as well. There was plenty to do in this community some 55 miles northeast of the Winona homestead. Pearl found lots of work. She delivered babies in town and throughout the countryside. She then stayed with each new mother until she was ready to manage on her own. When Pearl stayed on after a birthing, she was responsible for helping to care for the baby and mother, as well as cooking and cleaning for the family. Pearl went home each day around noon to check on the children and see what trouble they had gotten into, but the younger children were being raised primarily by 12-year-old Charles, Jr. and Nita, age 10. When Pearl wasn't delivering babies, she stayed busy cleaning households, sewing, or cooking for other families, helping to doctor the ill, and selling garden vegetables to the local grocers and restaurant owners. She was always working to bring more money into the household to keep the children in food and clothing and save toward her goals. During an epidemic of typhoid fever, Pearl stayed with a quarantined family because, as a child, she had contracted the disease and was therefore immune. Dr. Palmer had discovered that the Simpsons, a family of five, had the malady. When Pearl volunteered the information of her immunity, she was assigned to the home. Pearl lived in the quarantined home for 2 months as she nursed the entire family back to health.

The kids were also working. At age 12, Charles already had plenty of farming experience. Local farmers were happy to provide jobs for him. Nita, at 10, was cooking, cleaning, and babysitting, essentially raising 5-year-old Delbert and 3-year-old Melvin. Chester was running errands for store and restaurant owners, and Don "Speck," at age 9, started his own newspaper route, which eventually fell to Delbert. The children were no longer farm kids. They were small town kids in the middle of farm country.

During their first week in town the boys were challenged by another group of town kids. A large 15-year-old boy confronted Charles, Jr. and informed him that his name would henceforth be Charley Gravy. Charles attempted to instruct the bully in the correct pronunciation of his name, but the boy did not recant. Chester ran home, but the other boys stayed and watched while 12-year-old Charles administered a sound thumping to the 15-year-old and offered a similar lesson to the others. From then on those boys were fast friends with Charles and never again called him names. The other boys did have a name for Chester, though. From then on, they called him Chicken Gravy, but never while Charles was within earshot. Chester always ran from fights. Speck and Delbert always tried to talk their way out of fights. Speck could always change the subject or entertain with thrilling stories, but Delbert had to prove himself a few times. Melvin, at only 3 years of age, was thrilled by Charles's strength and fighting ability, so he tried to look for fights. As he grew up, he never started fights but always welcomed them. However, as a young boy, nobody wanted to take on such a small tyke, and seldom did anyone want to fight Charles Gregory's youngest and smallest brother.

Charles soon learned that the bully who had confronted him wasn't the toughest boy in town. That honor fell to Laverne Marple, a quick, wiry pugilist. When the Marple boy heard about newcomer Charles, he looked all over town for him. When he found Charles, Laverne asked him if he thought the name Laverne was a sissy name. Charles, not really looking for a fight, responded with a firm "No!" Laverne pushed Charles! Chester ran home. Mel jumped on Laverne. Speck and Delbert pulled Mel off the challenger, and the fight ensued. It was a long, bloody bout, but in the end Charles stood over the Marple boy. After that they were always best of friends, and the streets of Oakesdale were thereafter safe for the boys. Charles and Laverne Marple played on the 2nd Place Oakesdale High School basketball team together. The two boys also used to hunt pheasants throughout Whitman County and fish many of the streams and lakes throughout Whitman and Spokane counties. In the years after high school, Charles and Laverne ventured farther north to catch larger rainbow trout, German brown trout, and cut-throat trout at Davis Lake, King Lake, North Skookum Lake, South Skookum Lake, Skookum Creek, and Davis Creek in Pend Oreille County. They also went to Sprague Lake and fished the inlet stream with Charles's old friend Ernest Loy. Sometimes the three young men went to the Chattaroy area north of Spokane and fished at Bear Creek and Little Spokane River. They were proud of those catches, because they would usually get a few Eastern brook trout. The brookie, not actually a trout, was a very colorful char with delicious, deep orange meat.

Now that little Delbert was off the farm and living in a town, he supposed he'd never acquire another wild pet like his carp. However, before a year had elapsed, his big brother surprised him with just such an animal. Charles, Jr. had been working for Ralph Littleton, a farmer with land just north of town. Charles's job was to remove the accumulated weeds from the rod weeder that Mr. Littleton pulled behind a team of mules. The last field was finished off early in the day, and Charles, Jr. was paid. Mr. Littleton reached into a bag and pulled out change totaling $1.25 and thanked Charles with the payment. It was much needed money for the family and good pay for two days and a couple of hours, especially for a 13-year-old boy. The young farmhand happily walked the 2 miles home and took a shortcut—the back way through Deep Cut and over three rolling hills. Near a stand of trees he spotted something peculiar. It was a large bird with an apparently broken wing. It appeared to have large eyes, horns, (actually ear tufts), a sharp beak, and vicious looking talons. Charles returned to the farm and borrowed a gunny sack from the farmer. He then headed back to the stand of trees known as a wood lot. (In this area for a few years there was a requirement to plant a two-acre wood lot as part of the homesteading provisions.) Charles, Jr. slipped his work gloves on and struggled to capture the menacing looking bird. He took it home and showed his mother. She wasn't impressed as Charles conveyed to her that it was a present for Delbert. Pearl informed him it was a great horned owl and it could be dangerous. Delbert pleaded to keep it, and his skeptical mother gave in.

Charles helped Delbert place the owl on a low rafter in the back of the wood shed. They clamped a 5-foot length of chain around its foot and nailed the other end to the rafter. Delbert was thrilled with his new pet. He filled a water dish on a nearby shelf every morning, and the owl would drink from the container. The town butchers often gave Delbert scraps for his new pet. He also gave it mice recovered from a trap, or a frog or a minnow from McCoy Creek behind the house, and occasionally he smuggled some of his supper out of the house for the owl. Little Del was exhilarated to have such a magnificent pet, and he was happy that his older brother was so generous with him. After all, this was the same brother who thumped Chet and Del whenever they failed to follow his directions.

The pet did have a distinctively annoying habit though, hooting loudly and sometimes throughout the night. When it was obvious that the wing had healed, Pearl announced that the bird must be freed. Delbert remembers that after his pet was released, it stayed around the neighborhood for about a week but finally left.

George Latimer, the father of Delbert's friend Al, was working a field for L. D. Johnson about 5 miles north of town, when he told his son that he had seen a mother coyote moving her pups into a den on a hillside a few hundred yards north of Sam Lathrum's farmhouse and south of the Fairbanks railroad siding. The next morning found Del and Al headed to the den with shovel in tow. They located the den on a steep slope, just where Mr. Latimer had described it to be. Cautiously, the boys tried to look into the den, but they saw nothing but darkness. They dug the hole wider, but still they saw nothing. Al wondered how deep the den reached, so Delbert took the shovel and extended it back into the den as far as he could reach. He thought he felt something move so he withdrew the shovel. It seemed heavier; and as he slowly pulled it out, there sitting up on the shovel was a little coyote pup. Thrilled by the sight, Delbert took the new pet home and kept it in the woodshed. He fed and watered it just as he had done for the owl. Much to Delbert's dismay, however, the pup was probably too young to be separated from its mother. It died after about a week.

Delbert's next pet was a little tamer than the owl and much more hardy than the coyote pup. Byrd Elnor had a farm about 2 miles east of town along Pleasant Valley and just past the Fletcher School. Byrd's hired man found a mother badger raiding the chicken coop and he shot the varmint. The dead mother's baby then followed him around and he'd feed it. The hired man put a small harness and chain on the young badger and trained it to leash. It was very friendly and safe, unlike a wild badger, which can be ferocious. One summer day when Delbert was fishing on Pine Creek near the farm, the hired man told him that he was leaving for a job in Spokane and he couldn't keep the pet. Delbert proudly walked home with the young badger at his side. He raised this large member of the weasel family to adulthood. It always followed Delbert and came to his call. Delbert could feed Badge by hand, but the badger hissed violently at anyone else. Delbert was very pleased that Badge was friendly to him and nobody else.

It was at this time that Pearl was working in the quarantined Simpson home. She didn't want Del and Mel to be a burden on the older kids, so for two months young Mel was sent to live with Fred Crowe's local farm family and Delbert was sent to his maternal grandfather, L. C. Johnson in Walla Walla. Nita was perturbed by the menacing badger, and with Delbert absent she gladly set it free. When Delbert returned he eventually got over the loss of the pet, but after a few weeks he found a badger walking along a roadside ditch south of town on Thorn Creek Road. Delbert was certain he recognized it. He called Badge and it allowed him to approach. Del took off his belt, placed it around his pet's neck, and led it back to town. The badger still recognized and responded to Delbert, but apparently it had turned too wild. One morning he found that it had dug a hole under the shed wall and left, never to be seen again.

The next pet for little Del was short lived. Chet and Del were working for Ralph Littleton one cool spring day. At the end of the day the farmer pulled out the last of his coins — a fifty-cent-piece for Chet. He announced to Delbert that he had something better for the young man. He left for a moment and when the farmer returned he handed the young farmworker a duck with burlap sack to carry it home. Delbert was euphoric and figured that he had the best deal ever! Chet had to tell Del to shut-up a number of times on the walk home, but Delbert was too excited to stay silent. When Chet and Delbert got home they showed Delbert's new pet to Pearl. He took the duck out of the sack in the kitchen. It promptly sluiced all over the floor. Pearl grabbed the duck, took it outside, placed it on the stump, and sliced off its head. Little Del was disappointed that he hadn't earned a pet — he'd earned supper for the day.

Delbert also had some other short-lived but equally beneficial pets. He sometimes set up a box in his mother's large garden behind the house. He'd scatter wheat beneath the box, prop it up with a stick, and tie a length of twine. With great anticipation, little Del then waited on the back porch for some of the abundant Hungarian partridge or California quail. Whenever he captured a bird or two, he put them in the shed as pets. His sister often checked the shed for the evening's dinner—roasted game bird! This was The Great Depression, and edible pets had a short life span.

Next, Delbert shared a semi-wild pet with his friend Wally Brundage. Wally and Delbert saw a male coyote hooked up with Wally's pet female English spaniel. Two months later the spaniel had a small litter of pups, but only one of the cross-breeds survived. It grew up as somewhat wild and looked like a coyote except that it had some large brown patches on its back. The boys proudly walked the strange hybrid canine around town on a leash. Delbert and Wally felt almost as if they were wild animal trainers.

Delbert had other wild pets over the years. He once dug a kestrel (sparrow hawk) out of a nest hole in a clay bank off the Hume Road. He fed it butcher scraps, but it eventually escaped back to the wild. He also had a mourning dove for over a year and a friendly, well trained pigeon for several years. Each day he let the pigeon out of the shed, and the bird flew around the town in a large circle several times and then returned to its shed. Delbert also obtained a crow and a magpie. He got the magpie from a neighbor's barn. Using a ladder and a flashlight, Speck and Delbert climbed up to a nest and raided the fledgling bird at night. The neighbor told the boys they could use a knife to split the bird's tongue and it would grow up to talk. They tried this and the magpie did make some strange noises over the next couple of years, but the bird never repeated any of the words they tried to teach to it.

At the age of eight, Delbert had a painfully traumatic experience. His older brother Speck had just finished wet-mopping the front porch. Delbert had been teasing his older brother Chet. Chet began chasing his younger brother around the house and when

Delbert tried to escape he slipped on the wet porch floor. Delbert plunged headfirst on the back of a metal axe head, painfully losing parts of his front teeth. The local dentist filled in the broken teeth with gold fillings. That earned Delbert the nickname of Goldie, but it didn't last past junior high school.

Unwittingly, Delbert suffered from another of Chet's antics. Before school one morning, Chet had an idea to make it an exciting day in school. He had a practical joke planned. Chet stopped by the Piggly Wiggly Grocery and purchased a carton of limburger cheese. When he got to school and as nobody was looking, the young humorist rubbed the smelly cheese on each of the radiators in turn. After a half hour, the entire school building reeked of a foul odor. The school superintendent called each of the groceries in town and discovered that one of the Gregory boys had bought limburger that very morning, but the grocer couldn't remember which of the boys made the purchase. The superintendent had already herded the children into study hall and when he entered, the stern administrator announced what he had learned. The superintendent's son stood up, pointed at little Del, and said, "There's a Gregory!" Delbert spent the rest of the day in the office. Nobody talked to him all day and he didn't understand what had happened. He didn't know why he was there or what had transpired. Although Delbert was adept at memorizing facts and figures, as he admitted years later, he usually didn't know what was going on at school.

In spite of the occasional accident or discipline incident, the boys did have an enjoyable childhood and found much to do in and around this small town. In the summer and fall they hiked along the creeks that ran through town. They could catch turtles, crawdads, water snakes, and frogs, as well as frog eggs, polliwogs, and tadpoles. Whenever they caught a large number of crawdads, they gave them to their mother. Pearl and Nita then pickled the tails and canned them. The boys also found fish in these creeks just like the ones near the old homestead. Sometimes they hiked out to the Fletcher School and fished in a large wide pool, which was part of the creek. This was also one of their swimming holes, and they erected a large diving board to increase the fun. Sometimes they walked out past the Seabury railroad siding to Red Bridge near the John Fox farm. There was a large pool below the bridge. When the boys weren't pulling out trout, they were swimming in the impoundment as well, and camping out for a night or two at a time. In the evening they built a fire and roasted the speckled trout, tinch, shiners, or catfish. During the winter they skated on some of these creeks, and to warm up they built a large fire next to any frozen pools or impoundments.

Once a year the Oakesdale Theater had a drawing of the accumulated tickets the patrons had purchased over the course of the year. During his 5th grade year, Mel won the grand prize, a bicycle worth an estimated $25, one of the best conveyances of that time. Early that summer, Mel and Delbert rode to Chacolet Lake, a south arm of the Coeur d'Alene, taking turns riding on the handlebars as the other pedaled. They were joined by their friend Ray Blair. Ray was recently from Kentucky and earned the nickname Tuck. The three boys traveled the 25 miles to the lake over dirt roads. They took bedrolls and plenty of gear, including their willow fishing poles. The boys spent three nights and had a great time swimming and fishing. On the fourth day, Charles picked them up in the family's 1928 Model-A Ford. Although the three boys had a great time, they were tired of eating fish and biscuits. When they got home the boys had cereal with fresh milk and raspberries. Delbert swore that was the best tasting refreshment he'd ever eaten.

Additionally, the boys always found plenty of work to keep them in money and able to provide a portion to their mother for the household. One of Delbert's jobs was as janitor of the Oakesdale Theater. He cleaned, swept, and carried out the garbage, and in the winter he stoked the fire and shoveled snow off the sidewalk. Sometimes his older friend Jack Elkins let him take a turn at running the projector. The boys also went around town in the winter and shoveled sidewalks and driveways for a nickel. But throughout their years growing up in Oakesdale they were farmed out at different times. While Mel was in high school, he spent 3 years working for

Fred Crowe. During that time, Mel stayed in the bunkhouse, did some morning chores, ate breakfast with the family, rode the bus to school, played sports, came back to the farm, did evening labors, and took his dinner with the farm family. Delbert also was farmed out to the Hobart Black farm in the summer and, during his junior and senior years in high school, to Sam Lathrum's farm.

The kids were also involved in school activities. Charles and Speck were outstanding football players. All the boys played football. During most years they played eleven-man football, but for a few years the school was in a six-man league. Most of the teams wore brown or grey uniforms, and the helmets were made of leather with no facemask. The boys usually wore a stocking cap under the helmet. Delbert recalled their six-man quarterback/running back Stanley "Sammy" Henrickson. He said the diminutive Hendrickson was fast enough to get away from anyone in the league, but often ran headfirst into the gut of the largest player on the other team just to knock the wind out of the opponent. That was his method of softening up the defense. During the eleven-man years, games were primarily defensive with low scores. One loss to the Tekoa Tigers was 0-3, but the lowest score was with Pine City, a 0-0 tie. All the boys loved football, but Speck was the only one who went on to play the sport in college.

In high school, Speck was a running back, but as a freshman at Whitworth College, he was starting tackle on both sides of the ball. The Pirates' last game of the season was with the Montana State College Bobcats. A strong Chinook—a warm wind from the west— had blown over the mountain ranges and into Bozeman the day before and melted the snow on the field. That evening the temperatures fell below zero from a polar express coming down from the northeast. The result was a gridiron that was better suited for hockey. That was Speck's toughest game. The harder he tried to run, block, and tackle, the harder he hit the ice. Speck realized that he was in a great deal of pain early in the game. His arms and legs were experiencing extreme pain. He played through as tough as possible and had over a dozen tackles. Late in the game at 0-0, Speck told the coach something was wrong with him. He spent the remaining few minutes cheering his team from the sidelines and trying to convince them that they could score. With seconds left, the Pirates of Spokane scored the only touchdown of the game. When Speck got back to Spokane the following day, he went to Deaconess Hospital in a great deal of pain. There he discovered that both elbows and one knee were fractured. He had played most of his last football game with broken bones.

Charles, Nita, Speck, Chet, and Mel all played basketball in high school. Charles was the most successful, as he started for Whitman County's 2nd Place team in 1934. Both Nita and Chet were team captains for Oakesdale. Mel was known for his speed and coordination. Delbert was discouraged with his junior high basketball experience, but he loved the game and became a spirited cheerleader for the Panthers. He recalled his favorite cheer: *Cantaloupe, muskmelon, watermelon rind, check that score and see who's behind!* Of course that cheer only made sense when the Panthers held the lead.

The kids participated in other activities at Oakesdale School. Speck was a member of the OHS Bodyguards boxing team, where he was quite successful as a featherweight. Nita was a member of the girls' baseball team, chorus, and the Oaken Script annual staff. Delbert was also a member of the annual staff and served as art editor during his junior and senior years. Delbert drew the graphics for the annual yearbook. He drew a particularly popular scene of a boy fishing on the banks of Pine Creek; and that drawing is used on the inside title pages of this book. He was also a drummer for Nelson's Rascals, the school band. In later years he became a renowned drummer for The Rhythm Rascals Jazz Band. The Rhythm Rascals played for dances and benefits throughout Whitman and Spokane counties.

In spite of the economic hard times for the family and around the nation, Pearl was able to save enough money to make a down payment on a mortgage for a recently foreclosed restaurant. Although the Corner Café, Oakesdale's largest, most frequented, and most central eating establishment, was still technically owned by the bank, Pearl was its proud operator. She had reached one of her goals, and she worked hard to keep the restaurant and achieve her long-term goal of sending her children to college.

Oakesdale High School Basketball Team, 2nd Place Trophy, 1934.
Front L–R: S. Moen, D. Walker, M. Henning, L. Marple. Back:
H. Hilson, V. Van Alstine, C. Gregory, Jr., R. Reid,
Coach Kennedy.

Charles, Jr., and Laverne with a few North Skookum Lake
rainbow trout, 1936.

Donald Farold Gregory
Bodyguards Boxing Team
Sophomore Year, 1936.

Delbert Eugene Gregory
OHS Football Team
Senior Year, 1940.

The Gregory brothers, Oakesdale, 1938. L-R: Mel 7th grade,
Delbert 9th, Speck 12th, Chet 11th, and Charles.

Junior High members of Oakesdale Band, 1936. L-R: J. Barber, J. Walker, Del Gregory, W. Franks, D. Russell, and S. Henrickson.

Charles Ralph, Jr., 8th Grade, 1930.

Juanita Arline, Senior, 1936.

Chapter 6

And Yet Another Joy and Sorrow

For this, our light and transitory burden of suffering is achieving for us a weight of glory.

—2nd Corinthians 4:17

After Charles, Jr. had graduated from high school, he continued to work for local farmers. He had been doing this since age 12, when he first arrived in Oakesdale. His tasks included bucking hay and straw bales, cleaning chicken coops, barns, and pig sties, feeding livestock, milking cows, driving horses and mules, eventually driving tractor, servicing machinery, and much more. Charles had developed a reputation for being an outstanding farm hand, but pay was meager, and he was often paid with farm produce; however, his mother needed all the help she could get to raise Charles's siblings and provide the things she wanted for them.

Pearl did save up enough money for Charles to attend Washington State College for a semester. Charles started out doing well in algebra and physics, but with this new freedom he soon found that there were opportunities for fun and excitement. He enjoyed drinking beer at the local bars and dating a few college girls. However, he got the most fun from playing pool. He discovered that he had a talent for the game and began betting on the contests. On many evenings, Charles came back to his apartment with an extra $5.00, but he soon found that there were a couple of better players who often took all his money slowly over the course of an evening. His studies floundered, and that was the end of his college career.

As the nation found itself mired in economic depression, locally things were difficult as well. Running the restaurant was becoming more cumbersome and less successful. It was hard to provide for the children, but they did offer up one advantage for Pearl—she didn't have to fill a payroll. Nita and her four younger brothers provided the labor force for Pearl to run her cherished Corner Café.

Nita waited tables. Speck helped his mother cook. The younger boys washed dishes, peeled potatoes, bussed and cleaned tables, ran errands to and from the grocery stores, and swept and mopped the floor after closing time. Pearl obtained produce from each of the town's grocery stores, and locally from farmers. She also kept a large garden that provided parsnips in the winter and dozens of other vegetables throughout the year.

Finally, a more lucrative opportunity came for Charles, Jr. There was a job opening from Oregon Washington Railroad & Navigation Company (OWRR & N Co.), later to be taken over by Union Pacific in 1939. The company was repairing and replacing tracks and building branch lines. They needed local laborers; and Charles, with his reputation for being physically powerful, punctual, and industrious, easily obtained a position. He was hired as a gandy dancer for a railroad section gang. A gandy is a 5-foot metal bar, similar to a crowbar, used by the worker to lift and place the rails in perfect alignment. In order to do that, the worker usually jumped up and down, bouncing the bar to move the rail into place. From a distance it looked like he was dancing, hence the term *gandy dancer*. The pay was much better than that of a farm hand, and it availed Charles consistent hours and a regular paycheck.

During that time, Charles developed a friendship with George, a fellow section gang member. George was a married man a few years older than Charles. They shared an interest in hunting and fishing and went often. Usually, they hiked along McCoy Creek or Pine Creek and bagged several pheasants. They were both expert marksmen, and Charles, Jr. developed an accurate eye with his father's Browning 12-gauge.

However, George did drink a great deal, and his drinking seemed to be increasing. Charles became aware that something was bothering his friend. An unspoken cloud of darkness surrounded George's life, and it seemed to be getting darker. George finally confided in Charles that his wife, Minerva Marie (Minnie), and he were having problems. At that time it was uncommon for a couple married for several years to be without children, and Charles suspected that was the problem.

Minnie's parents lived across the street and down the block a few houses from Pearl and the kids. Charles noticed that Minnie seemed to be living there with her parents. When asked about that, George confided that Minnie and he had a bad fight one night after George had spent several hours at some of the local saloons in town. George said he couldn't remember what had happened, but Minnie moved out; they were separated and would soon divorce.

As Charles, Jr. saw more of Minnie in the neighborhood, he became fond of her. She had coal black hair and deep brown eyes with fair skin and fine features. He felt that she was the kindest, most beautiful woman he had ever known. Although Minnie was still legally married, Charles became extremely attracted to her. Charles, like others, assumed that Minnie was barren and perhaps that was the reason for George's sullen, intoxicated, and subsequent violent behavior. George had quit work and was continuously drunk and fighting in the bars. Charles hadn't seen him in months but heard of his out-of-control behavior.

Over the next year, Charles and Minnie saw each other often. When Charles got home from work, Minnie was there to greet him. They were together every evening, and finally they started spending nights together at one or the other's parent's home on a regular basis. They talked about marrying after the divorce from George became final. After a few more months, it was evident that Minnie was with child. Pearl, a highly experienced mid-wife (or mid-nurse as they called them back in those days), oversaw the delivery of Minnie's baby. Pearl had delivered several babies when she worked for Dr. Henry in the Endicott-Winona area; she delivered several more for the members of her Texas Draw Community Club; and here in Oakesdale, she delivered many more for Dr. Palmer and Dr. Hurst. This delivery was different, though. Minnie told Pearl what she had already suspected—Charles was the father of this baby. Pearl realized that she was delivering her first born grandchild. There was another difference though—a second baby came forth. The two twin girls were born only a few minutes apart, and Pearl thought they seemed to be identical. The only difference she could ascertain was that the first girl had a caliche or crown on the left side of her head and the other on the right.

Charles and Minnie were happy but uncertain about the future. The railroad work was finished, and Pearl finally couldn't make the mortgage payments on the restaurant. The bank foreclosed on her dream, just as it had done on the farm 12 years earlier. Although Pearl was able to work for Mr. and Mrs. Robert Lee at the Kozy Inn & Café and IGA, times were still difficult. For Charles, the only work he could find was as a farm hand. Again, his pay was meager.

Then, unexpectedly, although Minnie hadn't seen George in a year, he showed up at her parents' home. It was obvious that he had been drinking excessively as he threatened Minnie and said that he hated both her and Charles. George informed Minnie that he would never give her a divorce and that he would kill Charles the next time he saw his former friend.

That evening Minnie's father was celebrating the birth of his granddaughters. He was exuberant and rejoicing raucously at the nearest downtown saloon. He was probably a little too boisterous and he didn't realize George was at a corner table. George had heard enough and rose to his feet as he stumbled toward the equally inebriated new grandfather. George plunged a knife into his former father-in-law's abdomen and then again into his right leg. George sped out of town as Minnie's father was taken to the family's home. Minnie's mother took her husband to the Deaconess Hospital in Spokane. His wounds were painful but not severe, and he was discharged after a few days. The family had enough of Oakesdale, and with George running the countryside on the loose; Minnie's parents decided the family would return back east to stay with some relatives. Charles knew that Minnie had family in Tennessee and Missouri, but he didn't know where, and he never heard from Minnie again.

Charles was deeply distraught. He was a man who had his childhood taken away at the age of 10. Due to Minnie's continued marital status, he was unable to marry her. And now, the love of his life and their twin daughters were gone, and there was no clear picture for his future.

With war waging in Asia and Europe, the U.S. was trying to build a stronger, larger army and navy. Charles saw an opportunity to get away from his heartache, travel, learn a skill in the Army Air Corps (Air Force), and make some type of future. Aircraft was the wave of the future, and private airlines were developing. At the booming Pan-American Airlines, many of the employees had trained in the Army Air Corps. Charles hated to leave his mother and the kids, but this was an opportunity to gain skills and send back a monthly allotment to the family. Pearl gave Charles her blessing and noted that Roosevelt had signed a draft that could force Charles into the army by October. By enlisting now, he could select the Air Corps and have a better opportunity to test for a beneficial MOS (military occupational specialty). He boarded one of the passenger cars of the Northern Pacific and was on his way to Spokane, where he enlisted—a broken man, but one with hope for the future.

Chapter 7

Up and At 'Em
September 18, 1940 – December 9, 1941

Give sorrow words; the grief that does not speak whispers o'er-fraught heart and bids it break.

— William Shakespeare

Before Charles left home to be sworn in on September 18, 1940, he dressed in his best suit—his only suit—and Pearl took some photos of Charles with the boys. Mel was starting his sophomore year in high school, and Delbert was a senior. Charles, as the eldest brother, held his heartbreak inside, and the three of them appeared happy for the new school year and for Charles's new opportunity. Pearl's other three children were in Seattle. Nita was married to Ray Miller, a farm boy from near Tensed, Idaho, about 10 miles east of Oakesdale. Speck and Chet were sharing rent with the couple. With increased production of the B-17 and plans for a high speed, longer-range bomber, Speck and Ray both worked on the line with 4,000 employees for the booming Boeing Company. Speck was proud of his paycheck, bringing in $29.67 each 40-hour week. Nita worked for the Aurora Greenhouse & Nursery, and Chet was employed at Society Candies.

Charles proceeded to the Federal Courthouse in Spokane, where he and his old friend from Sprague, Ernest Harold Loy, raised their right hands and made the following pledge:

I do solemnly swear that I will support and defend the Constitution of the United States against all enemies, foreign and domestic; that I will bear true faith and allegiance to the same; that I take this obligation freely, without any mental reservation or purpose of evasion; and that I will well and faithfully discharge the duties of the office on which I am about to enter. So help me God.

All the new soldiers were paired and put up in the Coeur d'Alene Hotel on Riverside Street. Charles's roommate was Francis Winifred Agnes, a 20-year-old from Douglas County who had taken the Great Northern from Wenatchee that morning. They were provided a government chit allowing them to have dinner at the hotel, and they were to take the Northern Pacific to Portland the following morning.

The two young men got to know each other by discussing their lives and interests. Fran was strong, stout, and powerful like Charles, but shorter. He reminded Charles of his youngest brother, Mel. Fran and Charles spent some time arm wrestling and discovered they were both adept at the sport. Fran told Charles of his fishing experiences along the Columbia, Wenatchee, and Entiat rivers, as well as Chelan Lake and the small chain of lakes around Rock Island. He told Charles of his work picking apples at 25 cents an hour, and Charles agreed that was a better rate than some of his farm work, but not as much as he earned while working for the railway.

Fran also told of the orchard owners who were plagued by deer. They had him thin out the deer herds, right in the orchards, that the ungulates had ravaged. Charles was excited that Fran would take him to the orchards after their tours were complete and they could harvest several deer. Charles also shared his many and diverse hunting and fishing experiences. The next morning, along with Ernest Loy and several other young men, they boarded the train for Portland. Charles, Fran, and Ernest had a long opportunity to reminisce about their youths and their lives in general. Time passed quickly as they especially enjoyed sharing stories of hunting deer and pheasants and fishing the lakes, streams, and rivers of Whitman,

Lincoln, Pend Oreille, and Douglas counties. As the Northern Pacific came to a stop in Pasco, Washington, they took on several more young men.

That's when Ernie, Fran, and Charlie first got to know the young 20-year-old Nels. Nelson Herman Quast was originally from a German-Scandinavian community in Minnesota but had traveled with his parents and siblings to Kennewick, Washington, when he was just in early elementary school. Nels saw the Army Air Corps as an opportunity to finally make a respectable income and travel. As the young men told of their work experiences, Nels shared that he had been working in the potato fields. He revealed that it was back-breaking work that paid only one cent per pound. As the four men articulated their stories, they became good friends and sensed that they had much in common. Charles discovered that at about the same time Nels and his dad were fishing the Snake River for steelhead, a large seagoing rainbow trout, Charles had been fishing the same area for sturgeon.

At age 11, Charles had spent a one-week vacation from farm labor to fish with his maternal grandfather, Lyman Charles Johnson, near Wallula, Washington. To catch sturgeon, they fastened a skinned chicken to a large hook and swung it out into a deep slough or backwater eddy of the Snake River. The hook was tied to a thin, strong, 10-foot length of cord, and that in turn was tied to a 30-foot rope that was anchored to the wagon pulled by two horses. When a giant sturgeon had the hook set in its mouth, L. C. had the horses pull it ashore. This was a common practice when fishing for the large, prehistoric looking fish and is believed to be the source of the term *horsing a fish*. Some of these fish were 10 to 12 feet long. Papa L. C. smoked the white meat of this bony-plated but boneless fish, and Charles got to take plenty home for Pearl and the kids.

The four young soldiers had many such stories of hunting and fishing to share, and they felt more at home when they were with each other. But together they were all eager to start their new lives and training in the U.S. Army Air Corps.

Charles had been aware throughout most of his life that his mother always feared for his safety. He was surely aware that this was a natural reaction to the fact that he was the first child born after the anguishing experience of Neva's early death. Therefore, when he had the first opportunity, early the next morning, Charles sent the following postcard to reassure his mother:

Dear Mom,   *Thurs. Morning 7:50*

> *Just arrived in Portland about 20 minutes ago. Will be leaving for San Francisco in about 30 min. Will arrive there at 7:30 tomorrow morning. Just finished breakfast. Am O.K.*

Love,

Chas.

The four new friends arrived in San Francisco the following morning and were transported to Hamilton Field, where they began their basic training. They were instructed in military history, customs, and manners. They were drilled in marching and trained in the old 1931 Curtiss P-26 fighter aircraft, an obsolete piece of equipment. They also fired for qualification with the .130 caliber machine gun.

In their spare time the young men discussed the world situation. They were aware that Japan had some type of conflict with Manchuria several years earlier. They knew Japan was moving farther south into China, but they saw the Japanese as no threat to American interests. They also knew that Germany had invaded several European nations. There was general agreement that they'd like to "dust it up" with those Nazis, but the young soldiers considered the Japanese as unfit for competition. Most thought the Japanese to be small and weak with extremely poor eyesight. How could they fly aircraft effectively or fire upon their targets accurately?

What the young soldiers didn't know was astounding. The island nation of Japan was determined to form the Greater East Asia Co-Prosperity Sphere, a political and economic union headed by

Imperial Japan and in control of the western Pacific and most of Asia. In 1931 Japan had invaded and occupied Manchuria and had political control over Korea. Starting in 1937 as Imperial Japan withdrew from The League of Nations, the Japanese began to ruthlessly devastate many cities in China, including the brutally infamous Rape of Nanking. They had taken over parts of northern Burma and threatened the Burma Road, which was used by the U.S. and Britain to provide emergency supplies for the Chinese. They controlled most of French Indochina (Southeast Asia) as well. In addition, they had moved on Thailand, the Malay Peninsula, and Formosa, and it looked as if the United States' Philippines, with its deep water harbor, the Pearl of the Orient, was the only obstacle in the path of Japanese invasion of the resource-rich Dutch East Indies (Indonesia).

Of course they had no idea how well trained the Japanese troops were and that they were extremely experienced since they had been fighting in China for 3 years. They also didn't understand the Japanese push for advanced technology that led to the Zero fighter planes, which were three generations ahead of the P-26s.

Additionally, most of these new troops didn't understand that Germany had annexed Austria and the Sudetenland region of Czechoslovakia in 1938 and, encouraged by the Munich Pact, gone on the following year to invade the rest of Czechoslovakia. The pact that British Prime Minister Neville Chamberlain had heralded as "peace in our time" actually encouraged further aggression by Hitler. It had proven what every small-town schoolboy had known: Appeasement to bullies only meant more bullying behavior.

Next, Germany had signed the Non-Aggression Pact with Russia, which gave Germany the western half of Poland. As their Fascist Italian ally invaded Albania, Germany went on to violate that pact by taking the rest of Poland. Then in early 1940, using the Blitzkrieg (lightning war), the Germans attacked to the north and then west using the quick air power of the Luftwaffe. They conquered Denmark and Norway, then The Netherlands, Belgium, and Luxembourg (The Benelux Nations); and in June 1940, France had surrendered. By the time Charles, Ernest, Francis, and Nelson had joined the armed forces, Germany had been bombing Britain for over 2 months.

Charles enjoyed his training and loved the golden countryside of California. He also liked the idea of taking tests and classes to learn new skills. The rumor was that his group would have some regular duty at Hamilton Field after basic training and after a few months would be sent to Alaska. Charles and Ernest were excited that they might have the opportunity to hunt moose and ptarmigan and cast a line for halibut and salmon in their free time. The boys never suspected that they would soon be issued suntan lotion and the group would be shipped out to the Philippine Islands. Charles sent the following letter:

Dear Mom,   *10/14/40*

Am getting along fine & having lots of fun. I've only got about a week and a half of recruit drill left before being turned to duty. It will probably be Military Police or polishing planes for a while.

I've had eight examinations already and have got an average score of 96%. Sometime this week I will take my Alpha & Mathematics Tests to see if I'm eligible to go to Technical School. Night school was started yesterday and I enrolled in algebra, mechanical drawing & blueprint reading. Our instructors come from Marin Junior College. I haven't had very much time to loaf, but now I'll have a lot less. Is there a loose-leaf notebook around the home & my old physics book? If there is, I wonder if you could send them to me. I'll reimburse you for the postage.

About 200 of us took a 25 mile trip to the top of Mt. Tamalpais this last Sunday. We drove to within about two miles of the top and then hiked the rest of the way. We climbed about 2000 feet in those two miles & boy was I tired. There was a fire lookout station & tavern right at the top. A person certainly could get a good view of the country from there. I could see about six or seven different towns, both Alcatraz Island & San Quentin prisons & miles & miles

*out in the ocean… It's about time for the lights to go out so I guess
I had better close & hurry & shine my shoes.*

With Love,

Chas.

*Headquarters & Headquarters Squadron
45th Air Base Group (Reinforced)
Hamilton Field, California*

Two weeks later, Private Charles R. Gregory, Jr., serial number 19-032-202, was assigned to the 20th Pursuit Squadron, 24th Pursuit Group, Army Air Corps. He was transported to Los Angeles along with Ernest, Nelson, Francis, and the other boys from eastern Washington. Then they boarded the *U.S.S. Washington* as the newly trained troops received orders assigning them to Nichols Field, Philippines.

The soldiers were handed postcards from the U.S. Army Recruiting Service. The top of each card read, "The United States Army—Offers qualified young citizens many opportunities for adventure, a career, education, and travel." The education had been cut short, but they were now embarking on an adventure and travel. Addressed to Mrs. Pearl Gregory, Oakesdale, Washington, Charles's postcard read:

Oct 30, 1940

Dear Mom,

*Sailing for P.I. in just a few min. from Los Angeles aboard the
S.S. Washington. Tell all the kids hello. I'll be seeing you in a couple
of years.*

With Love

Chas.

Five days later the ship docked at Pearl Harbor in Hawaii. Charles wrote his mother again and told her he was having a swell time, but he had been a seasick boy for the first 2 days. He said he'd never seen such a beautiful paradise. He also told her that after

3 days' shore leave, only the 177 members of the Pursuit Squadron would re-board the ship. From there they were to travel to Shanghai, China, to pick up 3,000 refugees; then on to the Philippines to disembark. While in Shanghai and anchored in the Wang Pu River, Francis, Ernest, and Charles went out on deck to have a short look at China. Shockingly, they witnessed a few bodies floating down the river, then more, and finally a hundred bloated corpses. Some of the bodies appeared to move, and they realized fish were lunging at and tearing the rotted flesh. It was as if the boys were hypnotized; they were unable to look away until they became sick to their stomachs. After that, they wearied of the Japanese troops who had caused these deaths, and they tried to forget the gruesome sight.

As the ship gently sailed through the South China Sea to Manila Bay and past the island fortress of Corregidor and the peninsula of Cavite City, Charles could see in the distance expansive Manila and Nichols Field. He stepped onto the dock at Luzon, the largest of the islands, looked around, and realized this was a paradise even greater than Hawaii. The wide streets were lined with well-trimmed trees and shrubs. Beautiful orchid-like white, purple, pink, and orange blossoms were everywhere. The cogon grass was ablaze with white plumes reaching out of the tall, reddish, sharp-pointed leaves. Towering bamboo and palm trees were everywhere in abundance. There were pink and lavender hydrangeas, and short-trimmed bamboo hedges lined buildings and streets. Prevalent throughout the city and the base were sweet smelling lauan trees, known as Philippine mahogany and used for decorative red plywood. There were banana, guava, jackfruit, and mango trees. Among the coconut tree husks grew beautiful white butterfly orchids. The sweet aroma of kamias trees was all pervasive. Also known as cucumber trees, they produced an oblong fruit popularly eaten raw or in jams and relishes. The Filipinos recognized the fruit as healthy to the endocrine system. These trees had long, pinnate, hairy leaves and small, sweet-smelling purple flowers that looked like orchids. Enormous acacia trees were also present, with their expansive trunks and healthy purple berries.

Friendly people, shorter in stature than typical Americans, were everywhere. Many of the Filipinos hadn't been so friendly a decade earlier, but in 1933 the Hare-Hawes-Cutting Act provided for an extent of independence for the Philippines, but with complete U.S. control of bases and U.S. tariffs on the archipelago's exports. The situation was further improved the following year by the provisions of the Tydings-McDuffie Act of 1934; 36 years after U.S. occupation of the island nation, the U.S. government had promised complete freedom and self-government for the islands by 1946. That was something the ancestors of these Malay and aboriginal Negrito people had never experienced following Spanish colonization in the 1500s.

Those happy streets were crowded with people, tables, and carts filled with fruits, vegetables, dried fish, and meats for sale, and carretelas — small coaches pulled by ponies — or small water buffalos known as carabao. Smiling children begged for pennies in the streets. Occasionally, a taxicab or car drove through the boulevards.

Charles had landed here in a dry November, but now in June the rains were prolific. It rained almost continuously in Manila, and sometimes the precipitation reached 20 inches a day. Charles wrote his sister and her husband Ray. The air corpsman told them that he had to be careful with his clothes. If left unattended, damp belongings could become moldy in two days. If the walls weren't wiped down every few days, they would grow a long, sticky, putrid mold.

By May of 1941, Charles had finished the base engineering school and was billeted as the crew chief for a P-35. By late June the P-35s were transferred to another squadron, and Pvt. Charles Gregory was crew chief for the much faster, more maneuverable Curtiss P-40 Fighter. They had gotten rid of the old P-26s and added 80 P-35s, 40 new P-40s, and 20 new, long-range, Boeing B-17 Flying Fortress Bombers. While five new barracks were being erected and a new 150-foot wide, mile-long runway was constructed, they were transferred to Clark Field north of the Bataan Peninsula and at the foot of the Zambales Mountains. It was rumored that they would be transferred to Guam shortly afterward. Charles answered a letter from his sister Nita and brother-in-law Ray, and his letter revealed his longing for the farming and hunting of Whitman County.

> *… But there are lots of rumors in the Army so I don't believe anything until I see it. If we had gone everywhere the rumors had it, we would have been to every spot in the world by now… I suppose there are swell crops around home this year. I just got to thinking it's almost the 4th of July and nearly harvest time again.*
>
> *Time really does fly over here; but still, it can't go fast enough to suit me. When I first got here I only had to do two years, but the government has changed that. We don't go home till we are due for discharge. Unless the international situation is settled before then. I hope the British & Russians polish off the Nazis in double time. Even most of the boys over here kind of wish we could get in a few punches.*
>
> *I went to the hospital yesterday and had a tooth jerked out. One of my fillings got loose and I didn't know it and she ulcerated. I never knew there was anything wrong till it started aching.*
>
> *Have you done any fishing this year? Boy how I love to get a rod in my hands again. I haven't had a hook in the water since last May, over a year ago. I'm sure going to miss hunting also. I guess I'll have to go out and hunt some wild boar or alligators…*

Charles was probably referring to the caiman, a small crocodilian creature that was abundant in the Philippines. He probably didn't hunt them, but he was curious about the hunting back in eastern Washington. Charles often asked about the events of back home and in Seattle. At this time Delbert had graduated from high school and proceeded to Seattle, where he lived with Nita and Ray. Speck and Chet moved into their own apartment, and Speck bought a 1933 Ford Coupe. Delbert got a job working with his sister at Aurora's Greenhouse & Nursery on Saturdays, and he worked with Chet for Society Candies Monday through Friday. When Delbert had free time, he spent it with his cousin Katherine Waddle Deal and her husband Bob.

Although Bob was in the Navy, he spent some evenings professionally wrestling, and Delbert was his manager. Essentially that meant Delbert held Bob's robe while the sailor wrestled. Battlin' Bob was always matched up with the same person, Tall Tex Porter, and the two young men practiced to make the action look real. Katherine and Tex's wife, Sheba, both bleached their hair blond and stood in opposite corners at the matches. They'd yell epithets and swear at each other. When Sheba called Katherine a dishwater-blond, the crowd always roared, and when the bout was over sometimes the two women would cuss, pretend to fight, and pull each other's hair. After each match the five of them went out to dinner and had a good laugh.

Back in Oakesdale the farmers were cutting clover and alfalfa hay and servicing the trucks, threshers, and tractors for the upcoming wheat harvest. Kids were running the streets by day with firecrackers, and they were waving sparklers and shooting off bottle rockets after sundown. Flags were hung along Steptoe Street and the OHS band led the Fourth of July parade. Pearl started a confectionery and bakery at the IGA grocery store. She made candies and pies, especially her popular chocolate walnut fudge, sweet cream taffy, and lattice-crust berry pies. Pearl was also relieved to receive her new dentures. Mel was bucking bales, sharpening cutter blades, and greasing machinery zerk fittings on Fred Crowe's farm.

Charles wrote his mother and asked about the kids and community. He asked for a subscription for the *Spokesman Review* to be sent to the Philippines. The air corpsman also queried Mrs. Gregory, "Could you send me some of that good cream taffy and maybe some chocolate fudge too?" Charles asked about his old fishing and hunting buddy Laverne. Charles wanted to know if his mother had heard from Minnie and what the situation was with George.

Most of the 24th Pursuit Group was transferred to Clark Field near Ft. Stotsenburg. Charles liked this area because it was cooler. Located at the foothills of the Zambales Mountains, its elevation was over 600 feet, while the warmer Nichols Field was only 5 feet above sea level. Charles was glad he was still working with his fellow ground crew members Ernie, Fran, and Nels, along with their new friend, Private Bob Mailheau, an adventurous, active, talkative young man from Hollywood, California, also with the 24th Pursuit Group.

But Charles did miss the bustling activity of Manila, and he especially pined for his new Filipina friend, Maria Dagdagan. Charles penned a letter to his brother Speck and said he had fallen in love again. He went on to remark that with her coal black hair, dark eyes, fair complexion, fine features, and gracious disposition, Maria reminded him of Minnie. Charles commented that she looked different from most Filipinos he had seen so far. Maria explained to him that she was a Mestizo; that is, she had both European and Philippine ancestry. She said that her father's parents were Filipino and Malayan, and her mother was a Creole (a person of European descent, but born in the Philippines). She explained to Charles that her mother's parents both came from Spain in the early 1890s. Charles told Maria whatever ancestry she had — it worked!

At Clark Field, Charles was still stifled by the heavy rains. Clark was much more rugged and rudimentary than Nichols. The surrounding jungles were thick, steep, and menacing. The barracks were crowded. They were sleeping in an unused aircraft hangar housing 400 men with only one foot between each bunk. There was no mess hall for the 24th Pursuit Group; consequently, they had to eat on the ground or standing and using mess kits while the mess hall was being built. They had to shave and shower using cold water. Charles took an air mechanics examination and he was trying to qualify for technical sergeant. Now making $72 a month and in anticipation of his increased funds, Charles set up a monthly $40 allotment to be sent home. Charles also got to return to Nichols Field with a two-day pass to Manila, where he met with the beautiful and congenial Maria. He then got a twin engine Douglas B-18 hop back to Clark, where several of the bombers were being transferred.

Over the next few months there was talk about the threat from Imperial Japan. There were emergency drills and training exercises on the few days when it wasn't raining, but there was no real sense of urgency. The situation was about to change, though, and it changed suddenly and drastically — possibly one of the origins of the military term *SNAFU*, which, in more refined circles, stood for "situation normal, all fouled up."

On December 7, 1941, Pearl Harbor was attacked by surprise. Most of the nation's military leaders were expecting an attack, but not that far from Japan and not that soon. The attack left much of the Pacific fleet disabled or at the bottom of the sea. Many bombers and fighters were decimated. Losing over 2,300 soldiers, Marines, and sailors, U.S. forces were badly crippled in the Pacific Theater. Most of the enlisted men at Clark Field were unaware of the attack. Some officers wanted to get planes in the air to attack the Imperial Forces at Formosa, but MacArthur wouldn't approve it.

The attack force from the Japanese-held Formosa was originally scheduled to depart at a time that would have had Clark Field bombed at about the same time as Pearl Harbor. However, fog on Formosa delayed the Imperial attack by 9 hours. When the bombers finally lifted off for the Philippines, they assumed there would be no element of surprise. MacArthur's reticence proved their fears unwarranted, though; he had misunderstood and underestimated the Japanese military both before and during the conflagration. General Douglas MacArthur had been an excellent World War I leader, and he was the first in his generation — and the youngest — to be promoted to Brigadier General. But at this time, political savvy and the ability to manipulate a complicitous press were the primary qualifications for promotion, and that was MacArthur's strong suit. The quintessential political military man had been promoted to Commander of the USAFFE (United States Armed Forces in the Far East). He had the ultimate and final say on all matters in the Philippines; unfortunately, his mercurial decisions proved fatal to thousands of Americans and Filipinos.

After knowledge of the Pearl Harbor devastation and when he finally approved our B-17 aircraft to take to the skies as a show of force on the morning of December 8, MacArthur didn't allow them to carry bombs. He did allow the fighters to patrol the skies, as long as they did not range too far from the field. He didn't know that at 8:45 a.m. the Japanese pilots had left Formosa, headed to Clark Field. Before noon, our P-35 and P-40 aircraft came back to refuel and were neatly parked wingtip to wingtip and facing the runway. At noon, while Fran and the other aircraft mechanics napped in the barracks after an early lunch and the ground crews were in the mess hall, Clark Field was put on full alert. Fifteen minutes later the soldiers streamed out of the buildings to see what was making the noise. It sounded like a continuous draw of the bow on a low G-note of a cello. The buzz was ominous. When they saw the sky was filled with aircraft, they wondered if it was more of our B-17s. Soon the bombs started dropping, the ground shook violently, and the air was hot plasma! The sounds were deafening! The earth trembled like gelatin as lines of bombs fell, each with 100 pounds of TNT. Charles heard Ernest scream out "Incoming—get to cover!" Everywhere young men were yelling. The field klaxon sounded a loud EEE-ahh, EEE-ahh! Black smoke was billowing up from the burning fuel depots. Years later, Nels confided:

> *A kid came running by and said, 'Nels, get the hell out of here!'*
> *and he kept running. We looked up and saw hundreds of these big*
> *bombers coming from the west and the bombs were already dropping.*
> *The first bombs hit right under our noses. Only three planes got off*
> *the ground, and we lost 17 pilots that day.*

As Charles and Fran ran for some cover, they saw a young blond-haired soldier down in a ditch writhing in a pool of blood. His bloody severed leg was lying off to the side. Another young man was missing his arm and then the most horrendous sight—shrapnel had decapitated one of their squadron members. They saw the blackened skeleton of a fuel truck completely demolished, and underneath its remains were two charred bodies. Those soldiers had mistakenly sought cover under the flammable, loaded truck. Pilots were burned to death in their cockpits as they tried to lift off the runway. Flames and rising plumes of black smoke were everywhere as aircraft, fuel depots, and ammunition dumps were exploding. The hangars, new mess hall, and barracks were barely standing, full of holes from bomb shrapnel. There was no safe place to take cover! It was quiet for a few minutes; then came the Zeros with their large red spheres painted on the sides of the craft. As they flew in low, Charles could see the intense, clenched, threatening faces of those pilots.

One Army pilot got off the ground with his P-40. He followed a Zero and attempted to shoot it down. The Japanese fighters were even more maneuverable than this newest generation of U.S. fighter planes. They were much faster and carried two 20 mm cannons and a machine gun, while the P-40 had but one .130 caliber gun. The P-40 was hit, and the pilot bailed out. As the American parachuted toward the forest canopy, the Imperial pilot slowly approached and fired a few rounds at him. The lifeless body, under the billowing silk, gently floated into the bamboo canopy below.

Four years later, Sergeant Ernest Loy and Technical Sergeant Nelson Quast told Pearl that the officers didn't let them know things were as serious as they were; right after the initial bombing, not one officer gave the order to return fire. They said they were only kids and felt like sitting ducks. After the bombers came, Zeros followed with strafing, and four metal hangars were all shot up. Nels shared that those bombs had been purchased from the U.S. a few years earlier.

During the strafing, Nels yelled to Ernest and Charles, "Where the hell should we go?" Charles shouted back that it didn't matter, no place was safe. After what they had seen, it was obvious that one place was as good as another. Soldiers were being slaughtered whether they headed for buildings or ditches or stood in place. It was all luck or the lack thereof, so they just stood there for a few moments. But Charles wouldn't wait for the order to fire; followed by Nels and Ernest, he stormed into the armory! They grabbed the .30 caliber Browning automatics and several magazines of ammunition, filed out the door and onto the field, and fired repeatedly at the Zeros!

Years later Nels told Pearl that Charles had brought one of them down, at least some victory for the Americans and the 20th Pursuit Squadron. Ernest shouted that more and more Zeros were coming;

and as the three of them ran out of ammunition, they dove into one of the shredded hangars. Most of the Army Air Corpsman had never fired handguns or rifles, with the exception of those from eastern Washington. However, Charles was an experienced hunter by the age of 10. For him, it was probably like shooting his Browning semi-auto-load 12-gauge at pheasants; the only difference… the Zeros were faster, but much, much larger targets.

Within a half-hour after the attack, the field was eerily quiet, but it smelled of sulfur, gasoline, and smoke. Wounded were transported to Ft. Stotsenburg's hospital, a few miles to the west. Corpses and body parts were taken off the field. Charles, Ernest, and Nelson helped carry the wounded. While at Ft. Stotsenburg, Charles waited in a long queue to send a telegram to his mother. He knew she was often worried for her eldest son, and he had always tried to reassure her.

The telegram was addressed to Pearl, but included a cryptic message, possibly intended for his brothers. It read, "AM OKAY DON'T WORRY SITUATION WELL IN HAND UP AND AT THEM EVERYBODY." Pearl and Speck had both heard the news on the radio. Pearl called Speck and read the telegram to reassure him that his brother had survived the attack. As the brothers were growing up, Charles, as the man of the house, had always been the first to rise, and always started chiding, "Everybody up and at 'em!" But Speck took the telegram's particular encouragement another way. As he hoped for Charles's continued safety, the second eldest of the brothers, resolutely determined but with his heart in his throat, went directly to a downtown Seattle recruitment office and signed up for the Army Air Corps.

Mel, Charles, Jr., and Delbert, Oakesdale,
September 18, 1940, the day Charles, Jr. left
to serve in the U.S. Army Air Corps.

Pvt. Charles R. Gregory aboard *U.S.S. Washington*
en route to the Philippines via Pearl Harbor,
October 30, 1940.

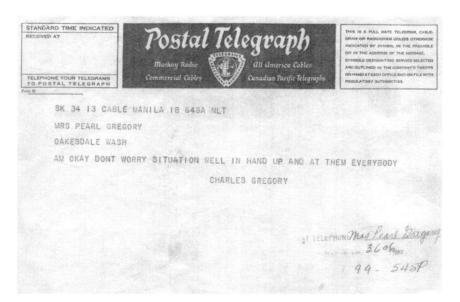

Dec. 9, 1941, the day after Clark Field was bombed and strafed by
Japanese, Charles, Jr. sent this telegram to his mother to let her
know that he was okay and included the cryptic message:
UP AND AT THEM EVERYBODY.

Speck heeded the call from his
brother's telegram, 1941.

Chapter 8

Abandoned in the Field

*Sorrow is better than laughter; for by the sadness of the
countenance the heart is made better.*

—Ecclesiastes 7:3

As Private Donald F. Gregory, "Speck," headed for Keesler Field, Mississippi for basic training, and while Mel, as a high school junior, was having his best basketball season ever, leading the league in steals, their eldest brother realized he was not just in an attack—he was in a war. Before December 8, 1941, Charles thought that he'd be headed home in about a year, but now he knew it would take much longer. He'd seen utter destruction of men and materiel, and now there was word that the other airfields and bases on the Philippines had been bombed and strafed as well.

The next evening after the bombing, Ernie and Nels, along with Charles, returned from their mission to help the wounded at Ft. Stotsenburg. After Charles had led them into the armory on the day of the attack—after what they'd been through together, fighting and downing an enemy aircraft, they seemed determined to stay close to Charles. That night after the return, the three men spent the night in one of the shredded hangars. They could see the stars through holes in the roof. The moonlight shone through, illuminating the hangar. "Where were the other survivors?" Ernie inquired.

The next morning gave them the answer. Men began wandering out of the jungle. At first just a few straggled out, then dozens, then hundreds. Fran spotted Charles, then others of the 20th Pursuit Squadron banded together. They discovered that over 300 military personnel and civilians had been killed or wounded during that first attack. After December 9th they were attacked almost daily, and the entirety of the Clark Field surviving personnel retreated into the Zambales Jungle and set up .50 caliber AA machine guns.

On the 10th, a few remaining B-17s from Del Monte Field on Mindanao, one of the farthest south of the Philippine islands, took off to head north, led by Captain Cecil Combs. They discovered that a Japanese troop convoy was headed to Luzon. Combs's men bombed the convoy and did some damage. On the return flight, Zeros attacked and damaged a B-17C flown by Captain Colin Kelly. Kelly was able to keep the aircraft level while his six surviving crew members parachuted to safety, but the plane burst into a ball of flames before the heroic captain could leave the aircraft.

Over the next 2 weeks, Brigadier General Clyde Selleck and his officers of the 24th Pursuit Group described the situation. There were attacks by the Japanese troops on the north shores of Luzon. Almost all the fields and planes on the island had been destroyed. The men were being ordered to salvage as much food, arms, ammunition, and medicine as they could find. MacArthur had determined that Battle Plan Orange was going into effect. That is, all Filipino and American troops would retreat to the Bataan Peninsula and hold out for as long as possible. They would need to transport all their scavenged supplies to the peninsula and bury them there.

The enlisted men of the 20th Pursuit Squadron were instructed by their officers that they needed to scrounge enough food for a month, maybe 6 to 8 weeks, and as much ammunition as possible. As privates Ernest Loy, Francis Agnes, Charles Gregory, and Nelson Quast were loading up a couple of deuce-and-a-half trucks at the mess hall quartermaster, Private Bob Mailheau drove by with a small convoy of men from the 24th Pursuit Squadron. He stopped and they exchanged stories and mission details. Bob's squad was headed to Manila, as per their lieutenant's orders. They were supposed to load their trucks with food to last 4 months, plus some medicine—sulfa, quinine, and Atabrine (a preparation of quinacine hydrochloride) to quell the horrific symptoms of malaria, but also used to treat giardiasis (an intestinal parasite that produces dysentery). Mailheau said that their officers figured the situation was much worse than suspected. The belief was that most of the Pacific Fleet was decimated. The U.S. would not send troops, aircraft, or ships to the Pacific if they had been earmarked for Europe. The U.S. troops on Luzon would be abandoned for an unspecified period. They were considered a write-off, expendable.

Charles and Ernest said they didn't believe that. After all, what was the first and most important rule of the U.S. military? *Never abandon troops in the field!*

Could everything have changed that much? Was their commander-in-chief so blinded by his devotion to Europe that he would abandon several thousand American troops in the field? Over the next 100 days they discovered their answer.

They formed a 15-mile line across the Bataan Peninsula, from east to west. This defensive front line stretched from the area of Mauban on the South China Sea to Abucay on Manila Bay—the Mauban-Abucay Line. Anchored in the middle of the line was 5-mile-wide Mt. Natib. To the north of Mt. Natib lay formidable terrain of rugged jungle and steep, jagged ravines. MacArthur reasoned that the Japanese Army couldn't make it through the jungles near the mountain. Within about a month, the American and Filipino forces discovered that MacArthur had once again underestimated the Imperial troops. As an added indignity, MacArthur and his officers and a large number of troops retreated to Corregidor. It was the island just off the southern coast of the Bataan Peninsula. Corregidor was heavily fortified and provided an underground maze of concrete and steel-reinforced tunnels and bunkers. It was supplied with hundreds of tons of ammunition, food, and medicine. The remaining 100,000 troops on the peninsula were left to their own devices. Within a month, as the situation became untenable, many

U.S. troops lost confidence in their absentee leader. A popular refrain sung to the tune of *The Battle Hymn of the Republic* summarizes the feelings of many such soldiers:

> *Dugout Doug MacArthur lies a-shakin' on the Rock*
> *Safe from all the bombers and from any sudden shock.*
> *Dugout Doug is eating of the best food on Bataan*
> *And his troops go starving on.*
>
> *Dugout Doug is ready in his Chris-Craft for the flee*
> *Over the billows and the wildly raging sea.*
> *For the Japs are pounding on the gates of old Bataan,*
> *And his troops go starving on.*
>
> *Dugout Doug, come out from hiding*
> *Dugout Doug, come out from hiding*
> *Send to Franklin the glad tidings*
> *That his troops go starving on!*

The 24th Pursuit Group headed to the jungles south of the Zambales Mountains, past the plains and into the rugged, steep, tree- and vine-tangled mountains—onto the steep cliffs and jagged ravines of the Bataan Peninsula. They buried their food, medicine, supplies, ammunition, and extra rifles. Besides the Browning automatics, Charles and his squad had scavenged old World War I helmets from a back storage room in the armory. They also took old, worn Springfield and British Enfield rifles and ammunition for the outmoded weapons. Many of those World War I rifles had their extractors worn down, and Charles had to use his locking gravity knife to pry the spent cartridges out of chambers. One was so flush that he had to fashion a whittled length of bamboo with cloth wrapped around one end to insert through the muzzle end of the barrel in order to plunge the shell casings out.

Although untrained for such a situation, Charles and Ernest, along with Nelson and Francis, had spent a great deal of their childhoods hunting and camping out overnight on their own. Ernest also had valuable experience from his years in the Boy Scouts. It was as if much of their lives had been spent preparing for this very moment. There was one other factor in their favor: All these boys had been hardened by difficult economic times—they were survivors of The Great Depression. Growing up on a scabrock farm in the middle of nowhere, Charles especially was hardened by tough times. He knew how to live off the land and make do with what was available. Having lived much of his life without a father or grandfather, Charles was also willing to make decisions and abide by them. Charles, along with the rest of the Flying Infantry, was ready. They were fighting ground troops without their aircraft. Their aircraft were all destroyed and their aircraft duties were gone. They had nothing left to do but become regular ground troops. There was also Sailing Infantry, not Marines, but ground-troop sailors without their ships. Deep in the jungles, the 24th Pursuit Group was not on the front line. However, in order to relieve the front-line infantrymen, they'd be sent north to the action for a few days at a time and then back to their makeshift camps.

At first, they lost a few troops each day in camp—mysteriously shot in the back. "Where were these shots coming from?" Nels asked. Fran felt they could be shot at any time without even seeing the enemy. Eventually they realized that the sniper fire was coming from caves in the steep slopes behind them. A spotter said there were dozens of caves, each holding dozens of Japanese troops. They started picking off the hidden troops when they appeared near the cave openings. Finally, the 24th Pursuit Group charged to the rear, up the steep slopes. They lost many troops while scaling up to the caves, slipping on the shale rock slides at the base of the incline, grasping for foot holds, and grabbing brush from the side of the mountain. They were being picked off by the Imperial sharpshooters, but the U.S. air corpsmen continued and killed most of the Japanese snipers. The Americans flushed out some of the enemy with sustained fire and grenades. Finally, a group of the Japanese troops ran from the caves, climbed to a precipice, took off their uniforms, and plunged to their deaths far below. Charles wondered what kind of people they had been fighting. What type of mindset did these strange humans have, that they would commit suicide rather than be taken prisoner? He later discovered firsthand that these men had been indoctrinated to believe that surrendered troops were lower than animals. They fervently believed it was more honorable to commit suicide than to be captured.

Nels wondered how the troops had gotten to these caves and where they had come from. The officers of the 24th Pursuit Group said there had been no paratroopers coming in, and there had been no landings from the South China Sea or Subic Bay. In later years Nels confided:

> We were unaware that 300 Japs were in caves behind our lines.
> We lost over 300 soldiers getting them out of those caves. We later
> discovered that those Jap troops had come from the University of
> Manila. They were posing as students. They were just waiting
> for orders to infiltrate when the time came.

After a few weeks, sustained winds were blowing from the north. With the winds came large swarms of the anopheles mosquitos. The Bataan Peninsula, with a plethora of creeks, streams, rivers, and swamps, was a breeding ground, rampant with these dangerous insects. Many of the females of this species carried the plasmodium parasite. Once bitten by the delicate insect, a person started experiencing the symptoms of malaria in 1–2 weeks. Charles and Fran contracted malaria and suffered in a fog of profound sweats, high fever, and delirium. Days and nights passed with very little activity from them. Nels and Ernest helped feed their friends and bring them water. After a couple of weeks Charles and Fran began to feel better, but this was short lived, for there were many recurring bouts of the illness for Fran, Charles, and eventually Nels and Ernest too.

The men also suffered from dysentery. The jungle was covered with swarms of black flies that feasted on defecation from open-pit latrines as well as the bloated, stinking, rotted bodies of the dead. Then the flies could just as easily land on the air corpsmen's food. As rations were cut in half and then halved again and again, and as the dysentery ate away at their intestines, the men were becoming emaciated. By March, Charles had dwindled from 180 pounds down to 105 pounds. He cinched up his belt to the last notch and then made another notch.

The 24th was being pounded by artillery and bombed from above. Imperial troops attacked in seemingly senseless suicide raids. The Japanese kept coming, and the Americans formed their front line farther and farther south. By January 22 the front line had moved south to the Bagac-Pilar Line. By February 13 the front line was formed to the Bagac-Orion Road. By April the defensive line had been moved south a total of five times; during the final weeks, they were retreating every few days.

Food was a problem, and by February each soldier had some rice that would be used sparingly and mixed with just about anything, even the inner bark of palm trees. By March 1942, the 20th Pursuit Squadron ran out of food supplies. At this point they were eating just about anything, living off the land. They gathered bananas, mangos, guava, and jack fruit with its nutritious pulp and seeds, and then they buried the fruits like treasure. Earlier they had been afraid of the jungle snakes, but now they pursued them. Charles tracked, killed, and ate pythons, smaller snakes, lizards, parrots, and large rats. Even the tiny split-toed geckos were thrown into the pot.

After the war, along with Ernie, Nels visited Pearl to tell her of Charles's final years and moments, but following that visitation he declined to speak of his experiences for many years. However, over 50 years later Nels shared this with Gaylen Willett of the *Entiat Valley Explorer:*

Keep in mind we had no food for 157 men in our outfit. We had seven cans of sardines and the cook made soup out of it, but he scorched it. It was horrible. We scrounged around, ate parts of the coconut palm trees and discovered a lot of things that were edible.

The monkeys knew where the food was and there was a big group (troop) of them in our area. One time, they had eaten all our stored bananas so my friends and I said, 'You ate our bananas so

we'll eat you.' We cooked and cooked them but they were tough. The
men also ate lizards and once, we cooked a stray cat for soup.

There had been a number of horses and mules on the peninsula. Those were eaten and none of the men complained about that meat. Carabao were butchered as well, but the small water buffalo tasted like the mud in which it had wallowed, even after being boiled for days. It was rumored that a few brave troops hunted caiman, small tropical alligators.

As the men were pushed farther south to the Mariveles Mountains, things were looking bad. With increases in sickness, malnourishment, diseases, jungle rot, infections, and rashes, as well as diminishing sustenance and ammunition — problems abounded. It is accurately estimated that 80% of the American troops on Bataan had malaria by April 1942. Furthermore, 75% were believed to have suffered from dysentery, and an estimated 35% had suffered from beriberi. The situation was hopeless. MacArthur had already been evacuated to Australia, and the nurses were evacuated as well. MacArthur had left Lieutenant General Jonathan Wainwright in charge, but he holed up on the island fortress of Corregidor, and Major General Edward "Ned" King was in charge on the mainland.

With their top leaders off the peninsula and with Roosevelt unwilling to send replacements or supplies, the troops realized they had been abandoned in the field. They began to refer to themselves as orphans or bastards. Many dubbed themselves as the Battling Bastards of Bataan. Some of these soldiers sang the following refrain, composed by Frank Hewlett, the one remaining news correspondent on the peninsula:

> *We're the battling bastards of Bataan,*
> *No mama, no papa, no Uncle Sam,*
> *No aunts, no uncles, no nephews, no nieces,*
> *No rifles, no guns, no artillery pieces,*
> *And nobody gives a damn!*

Surely, Charles knew that his mother and brothers gave a damn, but there was no way for him to find out definitively, and that perceived lack of knowledge probably hurt Pearl more than anyone.

Charles and the remaining troops on the peninsula were starving and running out of ammunition. The U.S. and Filipino troops put up a last stand on Mt. Samat. They were overwhelmed with bombs and heavily pounded with artillery, including large 150 mm and even 240 mm Howitzers. Lieutenant General Masaharu Homma's Japanese 14th Army won the final charge on April 8, 1942. Wainwright gave the order to attack the encroaching forces to the west, but with dwindling ammunition, and outflanked, it would have been certain suicide.

On his own recognizance, Ned King, an honorable man of the south, not wanting to lose any additional troops, in the tradition of his beloved Robert E. Lee, gave the order to surrender. The Battle of Bataan was the first land battle of World War II. It was also history's largest surrender of troops under the U.S. flag. King gave the order to destroy the remaining ammunition and weapons and fly white flags. Charles and the remaining members of the 20th Pursuit Squadron pulled the firing pins from their automatics and threw them away, and then they wrapped the rifles around trees.

The U.S. troops began the surrender. At the farthest point south of Mariveles, Charles, Ernest, Fran, and Nels staggered onto the Old National Road with their hands up. The enemy appeared to be in disarray as their cacophony of chattering arguments abounded. Thousands of troops were surrendering. An estimated 13,000 Americans and 65,000 Filipinos were surrendering to the Imperial Japanese Forces. An estimated 2,000 Americans and 20,000 Filipinos had lost their lives since the initial attack on December 8, leaving about 78,000 troops for the Japanese to receive. The Imperial Army planned a surrender not to exceed 25,000, so they were unprepared for this larger number of prisoners. They were also angry that this battle had lasted two months longer than their Tokyo commanders had been assured.

The Japanese set the tone for this surrender. They started forcing the Americans to their knees and taking their possessions. Watches, compasses, coins, and anything else of value was taken. Some officers and enlisted men wouldn't give up their wedding rings. The Imperial guards cut off their fingers and then took the rings. Guards also checked the prisoners' mouths for gold fillings, and those teeth were yanked out. The U.S. and Filipino troops were forced to sit in the sun for two days without food or water. There were prisoners up the road for several miles, but Charles was at the farthest southern point. The Japanese troops were constantly bickering with each other. Ernest and Nels later learned that the Imperial Army troops were arguing over whether or not they should shoot the prisoners to lower the number for which they would be responsible.

Eventually they were started on a long march, a march of some 70 miles. First they were organized on the road into groups of 40 — columns four abreast and ten deep, with about 10 yards between each column to minimize communication among the American prisoners. A large number of Filipinos were taken into the woods at bayonet point. Charles heard shots, screams of pain, and finally nothing. Ernest said he thought they were executing the Filipino scouts. He thought they were shooting some and bayoneting others. The thought was too barbarous for Nels and Charles to believe. It was an inhumane violation of the Geneva Convention. Further shock ensued when the Imperial guards returned. An officer protested the events, and he was immediately run through with a bayonet. Another soldier who lunged at this small murderer was severely beaten, then forced to his knees. An Imperial officer stood over him, drew his sword, pulled it back as far as he could, and severed the protester's head. Someone 10 yards ahead of Charles and Ernest — it was their old friend Bob Mailheau — yelled out in anger. A guard promptly struck Bob with the butt of his rifle on the back of the head. Blood squirted and then trickled down his bare back. Bob wobbled, but then stood resolutely in silence. All the Pursuit Group troops could understand that this was deadly serious.

There was no law, no order, no mercy, and certainly no humanity. The Japanese could do as they pleased. The rules of war were gone. Although a Japanese diplomat had signed the Geneva Convention, the Imperial Japanese government never ratified it. Many Japanese military officers and enlisted men felt the rules did not apply to them. They believed the vanquished troops had no honor—they were little more than dogs.

Prodded on by bayonets, the procession was forced to move forward. It looked as if the forced march was going to be a death march. After several hours a man fell next to Bob up ahead. The man was shot. Another soldier fell, and his friend helped to pick him up. Both were run through by the bayonet to the hilt. The other prisoners continued to trudge on, one step at a time, in stifling heat, along the dry, dusty road. Through his blurry vision, Charles saw a man on the left fall. A truck rushed up and ran over him. Was any of this real, or was this some horrific hallucination? Charles realized that he must continue, he mustn't collapse, and he must stay up and not fall behind—he must survive!

Then suddenly, as they were on a corner, guards couldn't see them ahead or behind and it happened. Mailheau made a dash for the bamboo! He disappeared into the trees and Charles could hear him breathing hard as he ran. There was no gunshot, no yell or sickening sound of metal penetrating flesh and blood. Ernest whispered to Charles, "He made it! That's the thing to do." Private Ernest Loy told Charles he was going next. Charles was suffering badly from a recurrence of the malaria. He said he couldn't make it. Nels overheard them and advised against it, fearing certain death. Years later Nels discovered that Bob did survive. He had run for hours and rested in a kubo shack used for tired field workers. When he awoke, two Filipino boys stood over him. They spoke English. The boys wanted to help, and they led him to a nunnery north of Guagua. Some nuns and novices from the San Fernando Catholic Sisters came to help him. Bob was diseased and emaciated. During the previous 100 days he had fallen from 150 pounds down to 82 pounds. A Catholic priest watched over him and brought a Dr.

Mario from the nearby village in Pampanga Province. When nursed back to health, Bob thanked his caregivers but feared his presence endangered them. He went off on his own into the rugged jungles. He met up with a few other American escapees and, although coming close to death a number of times, Bob became an active member of the field-named 155th Guerilla Group led by Major Clay Connor. For 3 years they spied on the occupying forces, sabotaged them, and passed on valuable military information when reinforcements finally arrived.

But on the death march, prisoners trudged on in the stifling heat. The sun burned white in the sky. Their tongues were swollen and dry — their lips were cracked and bleeding. Off to the right was a carabao wallow with green and brown stinking scum-covered water. A fellow prisoner flopped down into the putrid sludge and began drinking, but he was bayoneted. They passed an officer on his knees and tied to a stump. An Imperial officer brought his sword down and quickly severed most of the American's head, but it fell forward and hung from skin attached at the front of the throat. They saw a man forced to dig his own grave, but they trudged on. The prisoners were dehydrating. In this state it was difficult to comprehend the gravity of events. Consequently, many men made decisions that would have obviously been avoided if they had been thinking clearly. Some men ran stumbling into the jungle while guards walked nearby, but those prisoners were immediately shot in the back. Some men raced for any water they saw and were bayoneted clean through. One man ran into a sugar cane field and was shot. Another man was lucky enough to grab a piece of cane close to the road. He chewed and sucked on the sweet cane and finally spit it out. The man behind him picked it up and chewed it until it was completely dry.

Captain Samuel Grashio of Spokane, Washington, a pilot from the 21st Pursuit Squadron, 24th Pursuit Group, was marching with a dozen starving air corpsmen from the 21st. Up ahead they saw a Japanese equerry, or horse handler, throw maggot and weevil infested oats to the ground. When they came to the grain the men scooped it up—dust, oats, bugs, and all; they were happy for the extra protein.

Then a Chevrolet truck drove by and a passenger reached out with his rifle and hit Ernest in the head. Private Loy had seen and experienced enough. After the truck passed and on the next corner he bolted toward the bamboo to the left! Private Charles Gregory quickly shadowed him. They ran through the jungle for what seemed like hours as Charles struggled to stay up with his speedy friend. They came upon a rice paddy. On a wooden dike they laid down below the high stalks of grain, shielded from sight. When they awoke, the two men got up without a word and ran again. They ran for about a mile through the wet paddy and into a sugar cane field.

Ernest and Charles stopped to grab pieces of the cane. They chewed and sucked on the stalks and felt the energy surging through them. They raced on. Finally they dashed into thick jungle and stopped by a cool stream to refresh themselves. They stayed in this area for two nights and pulled large banana and nipa leaves down to cover themselves. The next morning they followed the stream farther away from the Old National Road. They came upon a dead carabao. It was stinking and ripe and covered with maggots around its gut and muzzle. Charles was too hungry. He pulled open its hide at the backbone and scooped out a piece of back strap (muscle attached along the backbone, aka filet mignon). As he retched, Charles gagged down some of the rancid meat. Ernest followed suit. They both took long drinks upstream and then began walking through the jungle again.

It went on like this for a few days. Then they heard a loud unintelligible cacophony of arguing. They hid in some thick brush and a Japanese patrol came by them no farther away than 10 yards. That was too close, and now they feared danger was around every corner. Then they began moving back south and down a ravine, cutting up their pants and legs on jagged rock. At the bottom they found a larger stream where they drank and bathed. Another night passed—in his malarial fog Charles had no idea how long they'd been gone. They went for over 2 days without finding food or water.

Finally Ernest yelled, "I found another stream!" As Charles came bounding toward him, he heard noises from behind. A loud crack resounded through the discordant jungle sounds—a whirling noise passed inches from his head, and Charles stopped running. Imperial troops were upon them and kicking and beating them! Charles took a heavy rifle butt to the clavicle and shoulder area. The pain was overwhelming as he heard and felt bone crack. The would-be escapees were marched back to the Old National Road, receiving numerous, painful beatings on the way. They rejoined the march.

Charles and Ernest recognized none of the troops with whom they were marching. Many were Marines, possibly from Corregidor. Charles thought he might have recognized a young man from his hometown of Oakesdale. Was it the old family friend and football quarterback Jack Elkins—the young man that he worked with, bucking bales of hay on Milt Silzel's farm? Charles was in too much pain, too disoriented and too dehydrated to speak. He could only think of moving forward, one step at a time. In his hallucinogenic state, nothing seemed real, but he knew he had to survive.

After a few more days of marching, they were loaded onto railroad cars at San Fernando. The doors were closed and Charles felt as if he was suffocating. It was too crowded to sit. He found a crack in the side of the car and attempted to breathe through the opening, but was soon painfully pushed aside. The air was putrid from men unable to control their bowels due to the dysentery. After another day they reached the village of Capas and were let out. The sick, dehydrated, injured, and befouled men continued marching. Before the day was over, they reached Camp O'Donnell.

It was a hell-hole. Its stench was that of rotted bodies, and open-pit latrines filled with dysenterial waste. Bloated bodies were stacked up outside the camp, and more bodies were being added to the piles. Men were prostrate and breathing—alive, but unable to move. The ground was covered in defecation from the dysentery. Men simply couldn't get up and move to the latrines. Charles, Ernest and the surviving prisoners in this group were forced to stand at attention for hours in the sun. Some of the men collapsed, but not one prisoner was permitted to pick them up. Then the Camp Commandant arrived to address the prisoners. Capt. Tsuneyoshi spoke loud and harsh. Through an interpreter he told the men that they should have died fighting or committed suicide. They had no honor and they would be treated like animals. They would immediately be executed if they disobeyed an order or neglected to salute or bow. He hammered home the point that they were a defeated, inferior race of cowards. It was not a welcoming speech. It further set the tone for their imprisonment and treatment.

Over the next 2½ years, Charles was transferred to two other equally sickening camps—Cabanatuan #1 and then to Lipa Camp #10B. It was 2½ years living in disease, extreme pain, sickness, starvation, and torture. Charles had survived the Battle of Bataan. He had survived the violent march, a thwarted escape to freedom for 8 days, and a return to the forced death march. An estimated 2,300 Americans and 20,000 Filipinos had been slaughtered on what was to become known as the Bataan Death March, arguably the deadliest and most inhumane incident of modern history experienced by Americans—American and Filipino soldiers, abandoned in the field, men left to die. United States War Secretary Henry Stimson told British Prime Minister Winston Churchill that the Americans on Bataan were written off. Stimson wryly exclaimed, "There are times when men have to die." There was no doubt—the troops had been abandoned in the field; it was a shameful and dishonorable act by the executive branch of the U.S. government in 1941–42! It should be noted that the Filipinos also proudly fought, marched, and died under the American flag. They too, were abandoned, both soldier and civilian. Charlie, Ernie, and Nels went on to survive the death camps for over 30 months before boarding the *Hokusen Maru* on October 1, 1944.

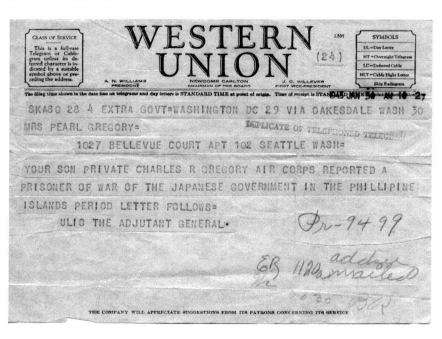

Telegram notice of Charles's prisoner status, 1943. After no word of
Charles's status for 13 months, Pearl was relieved that
her eldest was safe as a POW.

Map of Luzon, Bataan Peninsula, and the Death March.
Cartography by Christopher E. Gregory.

Chapter 9

The Death March Answered

… but we also exult in our tribulations, knowing that tribulation brings perseverance; and perseverance, proven character, and proven character, hope…

—Romans 5:3-4

It was late April, 1942, and Charles had survived much, but now he languished near death as a prisoner of war at Camp O'Donnell—badly injured, diseased, near starvation, and beaten daily. But thankfully, he had his old friend Ernie Loy to bolster his spirits, and the two men probably wouldn't have survived without each other's assistance.

Back in Oakesdale, Pearl was frantically writing letters to Charles. Each one was returned with the words "RETURNED TO SENDER SERVICE SUSPENDED" stamped on the front of the envelope. Her friend Grace Elkins experienced the same as she also initiated a frenzied letter-writing campaign to her son Private Jack Elkins of the U.S. Marine Corps. Jack had been stationed on the besieged island of Corregidor. He had grown up as a friend of Pearl's sons and had played football with Speck, Chet, and then Delbert. Jack was also languishing in disease and starvation, but he had been sent to one of the three Cabanatuan Prison Camps.

Speck's Answer

By the end of April, Pearl's second oldest son, Donald, a.k.a. "Speck," had completed his basic training at Keesler Field, Mississippi, and was one of five trainees promoted to private first class. PFC Donald F. Gregory was transferred on to Lowery Field for Armament and Gunnery School. Speck had grown up hunting deer and game birds, and he was already adept with firearms. Consequently, he excelled and was promoted to corporal.

His trainings had been so successful that he was granted the opportunity to choose his next schooling. He chose the 2nd Air Corps Radio School located at Washington State College in Pullman, Washington. He was back in Whitman County and had the opportunity to visit and console his mother and youngest brother, Mel. Mel would have nothing to do with consolation. His oldest brother Charles had always told him, "Never, under any circumstances, try to start a fight, but never back down from one." The youngest brother was always ready for a fight and this was a big one he didn't want to miss. He headed north to Spokane and attempted to join the U.S. Army. At age sixteen, he was told to go home.

On leave from the WSC Radio School, Speck, along with Mel, visited family friend Bud Haire. During that visit, Speck noticed a beautiful, young woman he didn't recognize. He had unknowingly seen her before, many times, years earlier when she was in grade school and junior high school. It was Bud's sister Ruth. She had long, flowing, strawberry blond hair and bright red adorning her full lips. He was instantly attracted to this fully grown and recently graduated young lady. Speck had only seen her previously in his peripheral vision, but now he stared into her eyes. In the past 4½ years he'd played college football, worked at Boeing, and served in the Air Corps. Ruth was also attracted to Speck, who was now taller, muscular, and slimmer and presented a striking figure in his military dress uniform. The couple dated and enjoyed their time together, and when apart they thought only of each other. Ruth agreed to wait for Speck's return.

By June, Speck finished his WSC schooling at the head of his class. He was promoted to sergeant and held the combined MOS (military occupational specialty) of gunner-radio operator. From there he was sent to Gowen Field near Boise, Idaho, for basic flight training. The air base had 6,000 trainees during World War II and boasted the nation's longest runway at 8,800 feet. At Gowen, Speck completed his flight training on September 13, 1942. Finishing near the top of his class, he earned his wings and another promotion.

Technical Sergeant Don Gregory was attached to the recently activated 347th Squadron, 99th Bomb Group, and received orders for transfer to Marrakesh, Morocco. His outfit headed to Morrison Field, Florida, where they were assigned to their Boeing B-17s. Their unit was called the *Diamondbacks*, due to the diamond shaped insignia painted on the vertical stabilizer of each aircraft. Speck's pilot named their Flying Fortress the *Stardust* and had the name clearly painted on the nose of the craft. They stayed on at Morrison and trained on the *Stardust* for several months.

Then Speck and his fellow crewmen, after receiving considerable training on their craft at Morrison Field, flew on to Borinquin Army Airbase, Puerto Rico. From Puerto Rico they flew to Georgetown, British Guiana (Guyana), then to Belem, Brazil, and then more than 1,000 miles over open seas to the Azores Islands. Next they traversed to Bathurst, Gambia, and finally rested in northern Africa in early March, 1943. Technical Sergeant Don Gregory trained on exercises as radio operator, but also as the waist gunner on the left side of their beloved *Stardust* B-17. After more training on their bombers, the group was transferred to Navarin Airfield, in Setif Province near Algiers, Algeria, and then the 99th Bomb Group was attached to the 12th Army Air Corps.

On March 31, 1943, Speck flew his first of 55 hazardous bombing missions. That first bombing was at Villacidro Airdrome, Sardinia, where they destroyed aircraft and ammunition dumps. Subsequent missions included bombing raids at Monserrato, Sardinia, as well as Gerbini Airfield, Sicily, and Foggia, Italy. At these targets they destroyed the German fuel storage sites, ammunition dumps, runways, airfields, aircraft, and aircraft production and assembly factories. After a few of these missions the hazard increased as the Germans began attacking the bomber squadrons. Until the last of the Foggia missions, only one injury had befallen Speck's fellow crew members. As a bomb hung-up on the edge of the bomb-bay doors, a crewman had the perilous duty to go down and wrestle it free. In the process, as the bomb fell, his wedding ring caught on a fin. He survived the incident, but he lost his ring and ring finger.

The most treacherous mission for TSgt. Don "Speck" Gregory and his fellow squadron members was their last at Foggia. An estimated 70 to 100 fighter planes attacked the convoy of bombers. Speck had always left the radio operation during radio silence and proceeded to the left waist gun. He had already received a unit citation for downing a German Fockewulff 190, and on July 22, 1943, he was in position and ready. They were attacked repeatedly by the Italian Macchi 202s and the Fockewulffs, but most of the hottest fire was coming from a squadron of highly maneuverable ME-109 Messerschmidts. The enemy seemed to be coming from every direction, one after another, each laying down heavy fire. Speck followed one after another, getting each in his sights and firing repeatedly. Finally, he made a direct hit and downed one of the ME-109s. His crew was credited with downing a total of seven Messerschmidts. During this 45-minute battle, one crew member was fatally wounded—the bombardier, the crewman in the most vulnerable position.

The *Stardust* was severely damaged, with over 50 holes in her fuselage, and the enemy had blown off much of the front and left landing gears. On approach back at Navarin, the crew sensed there would be trouble and they braced themselves for a crash landing. The remnants of the left and front landing gears descended, but the B-17 spun off the runway and pitched forward. In what could have been a deathtrap to the crew, not one member was injured in the landing mishap. Speck was proud that the craft they had flown and survived in was one of the B-17s that he had helped build during his 2 years working at Boeing Company in Seattle.

After the crash landing, the crew was rotated back to the states. Speck was assigned back to Gowen Field, where he helped train new recruits. He received his second unit citation for downing an enemy aircraft. Speck also received the prestigious Presidential Medal and the esteemed Air Medal with eleven oak leaf clusters.

Chet's Answer

Chester had always avoided fights. As a child he always ran from fights. He did play football and basketball at Oakesdale High School, and he excelled at those sports. In football there was a great deal of rough contact with little protection, and Chet was active on both sides of the ball. Although there was violence that he never avoided in football, there were rules and organization to the game. Perhaps his avoidance of street fights and schoolyard brawls was due to the uncertainty of outcome and the lack of rules. Perhaps he felt the same way about war.

In any event, Chet had no intention of joining the military. His help came from his work efforts. He began working at Boeing the week after Speck joined the Army Air Corps. He worked on the line to build the B-17 bombers and eventually helped produce the new long-range Boeing B-29 Bomber.

These were the craft that helped end the war. They were used to drop fire bombs on armament and ammunition plants throughout Japan. On March 10, 1945, they destroyed much of Tokyo with fire bombs, killing over 100,000 people. But when the Japanese government, led by Tojo and his equally fanatical militarists, refused to surrender, the atomic bomb was used. First, on August 6, 1945, the *Enola Gay* B-29 dropped the highly destructive bomb on Hiroshima. The Imperial military still did not surrender. Three days later, another atomic bomb was dropped on Nagasaki. Finally, the Japanese agreed to surrender on August 14, 1945.

Del's Answer

In April 1942, as Charles was forced to the Bataan Death March, Delbert returned from his Seattle work and enrolled in the machinist course at Spokane Trade School. His intention was to obtain a position at Boeing after successfully completing the course. However, Delbert was offered a position at the Spokane Army Air Depot (SPAAD), Galena Field, near Spokane. He worked there for a few months as a mechanic on Pratt-Whitney aircraft engines. But by November, Delbert was determined to follow the lead of his two eldest brothers. Del was profoundly aware of his mother's anguish at Charles's predicament, and he felt the only answer was to enter the fray. Along with his childhood friend Al Latimer, Delbert proceeded to the Army recruiter in Spokane and entered the U.S. Army Air Corps. On November 6, 1942, Private Delbert Eugene Gregory and Private George Allen Latimer boarded the Great Northern in Spokane and traveled to Fort Lewis near Tacoma, Washington, for their orientation and then basic training.

Del's younger brother Mel also tried again to join the Army Air Corps, then the Marine Corps, and finally the Army. Each time he was rejected as too young. However, the Army recruiter told the persistent, would-be soldier that if he had written permission from a parent or guardian, he could join. Mel spent the next month trying to convince Pearl to grant that permission, but already having three sons in the military, she was wary of consenting to his request.

At the same time Delbert headed for basic training, his fiancée, Nina Lee Littleton, and her friend Jean Beaman headed to Spokane to enter the same training that Delbert had completed at Spokane Trade School. After Nina and Jean finished the Machinist School training, they were offered aircraft engine mechanic positions at

SPAAD. The young ladies dubbed themselves "The Grease Monkeys" and worked for the Galena Field Engine Assembly and Repair over the next 2 years. Nina was a regular "Rosie the Riveter" as she worked on the Pratt-Whitney Hornet R-1690 radial, air-cooled, 9-cylinder engines for the Flying Fortress, Boeing B-17 Bomber. She also repaired and assembled the Bell P-63 Fighter engines. During this time, Nina and Del continued an ongoing correspondence.

When Delbert finished near the head of his class in basic training, he was one of six members promoted to the rank of private first class. From there he was transferred to Marana Air Field, near Tucson, Arizona, on December 18, 1942. At Marana, PFC Del Gregory completed Ground Crew and Basic Radio Training on the single-engine BT-13. He also completed Small Arms and Gunnery Training. In March 1943, Delbert was sent to Scott Field near East St. Louis, Illinois, for ROM (Radio Operator and Mechanics) training. During that 6-month period he was also temporarily stationed at the Camp Lincoln FBI Firing Range near Springfield, Illinois, where he qualified on the Springfield rifle and the .30 caliber Browning automatic. During May of 1943, his outfit was sent to sandbag the flooded Mississippi River north of St. Louis, Missouri. They were assigned an area east of the Cahokia Mounds (remnants of ancient Native American structures). There was no sand in the region, so they sandbagged clay dirt. In September 1943, after completing his assignment at Scott Field, Delbert was transferred back to Marana Field to complete more flight training with ground crew, mechanic, and radio operator assignments. It was during this time that Delbert and a friend traveled north of Tucson to the Verde River for several successful duck- and goose-hunting expeditions.

However, events started to become more fast and furious for Delbert by January 1944, when he was transferred to Kirtland Airbase near Albuquerque, New Mexico. He began having daily training flights on the B-24 Bomber, and they flew all over much of the southern United States on those exercises. During Delbert's Kirtland training, the British head of the China-Burma-India Campaign, Lord Admiral Louis Mountbatten, convinced the U.S. Joint

Chiefs of Staff that the British needed a large unit of cargo carriers in India—cargo carriers that would receive heavy combat. Lord Mountbatten was able to make this argument based on the recent incursion of the Japanese into Imphal, India. Also, it was important for the U.S. to keep the Chinese in supplies in order for them to occupy the Japanese Army. There was a fear at this time that Generalissimo Chiang Kai-shek, leader of China's Nationalist Party, was considering surrender terms with Generalissimo Tojo, leader of the Japanese militarists. After the Japanese controlled the Burma Road, supplies were cut off to China. It was thought that this air cargo supply was necessary to keep China in the war and on the side of the Allies. In later years it was determined that Chiang Kai-shek never would have agreed to any of Tojo's terms, but in early 1944 the U.S. wasn't convinced. This long-term air lift of cargo was dubbed the Bond Project and remained top secret information.

So when Delbert was promoted to corporal in May 1944, he had no idea of his future missions. Then he received orders to be transferred from Kirtland. The orders stated that he was to proceed directly, without delay, to Morrison Army Air Field, near West Palm Beach, Florida. At Morrison, the 3rd Combat Cargo Group was formed. It was provided with 100 twin-engine Douglas C-47 aircraft, and the group were divided into the 9th, 10th, 11th, and 12th Combat Cargo Squadrons, each with 25 of the Douglas aircraft.

Cpl. Delbert E. Gregory was assigned as a radio operator for one of the C-47s of the 11th Combat Cargo Squadron. After performing exercises on their twin engine plane, on May 22, 1944, they flew on to Borinquin Field, Puerto Rico, without knowing their itinerary. In mid-flight, the pilot, 1st Lt. John J. "Luke" Lukaszcyk (pronounced *Loo-car-chek)*, was allowed to open the orders and inform Delbert and the other crew members of the 3rd Combat Cargo Group's assigned destination—Sylhet, India (Bangladesh), and that the 11th Squadron's final station was Dinjan Airfield, India. After spending the night at Borinquin, they departed for Georgetown, British Guiana (Guyana), Belem, and then Natal, Brazil. From Latin America they flew over water for 1,448 miles, an 8-hour flight to the tiny

Ascension Island in the South Atlantic. Ascension was only 34 square miles and 1,000 miles from the nearest airfield near Accra. Accra, British West Africa (Ghana), was reached, and each aircraft's navigator, on loan from the Army Transport Command, departed the convoy. From Accra and thereafter, Delbert acted as radio operator and navigator of his craft. He headed on to Kano, Nigeria, then on to El Fashier, Egypt; and before leaving the Dark Continent they landed briefly in Khartoum, Egypt (Sudan). Then in the Mideast they flew to Aden, South Arabia (Yemen), and Masira Island, off the coast of Oman. From Masira they traversed the Arabian Sea; and on April 1, 1944, the 3rd Combat Cargo Group arrived in Karachi, India (Pakistan) near the northernmost of the mouths of the Indus River. After spending the night in Karachi, they proceeded to Agra, India, where they rested for two days. During that time they were able to tour the city and visit the breathtaking Taj Mahal. From Agra they flew on to Sylhet, India (Bangladesh), on the flood plain of the Ganges River; and flying from Sylhet, the 11th finally rested at their destination in Dinjan, India. All the members of Delbert's crew were in awe that they had just traveled halfway around the world in 14 days.

By the end of the journey, 96 of the original 100 C-47s arrived intact. Two of the craft had engine trouble while on the ground, and the crew members eventually were transported to Sylhet in order to reinforce personnel. One aircraft of the convoy had mechanical problems at the mouth of the Amazon River and violently crashed on one of the delta islands, and all five crew members lost their lives. Another C-47 of the 3rd Combat Cargo Group was plagued with mechanical failures and went down in the Thar Desert between Karachi and Agra. All four members of that crew perished as well.

Upon Delbert's arrival at Dinjan Airfield, the 11th was billeted in bashas. Those were native-built huts made of bamboo walls with grass thatched roofs. The crewmen had 2 days to acclimate themselves while their pilots winged with experienced ATC flyers in order to ascertain the routes. On the third day, Delbert's C-47-357 was back in the air and transporting rice, dahl, and atta (cereal grains), loaves of bread for U.S. troops, and canned hardtack and rum for the British troops. Those supplies were flown into Burma at the newly constructed runway at Myitkyina, pronounced *mitch-i-now*. Delbert's crew consisted of the crew chief and engineer Cpl. Bill Looney, co-pilot 2nd Lt. John Macabee, and of course 1st Lt. Luke.

After just a few flights, Luke discussed a problem with the crew. On every mission, their craft was always overloaded, and it was difficult to control the cargo carrier. Consequently, they needed to discover a way to decrease the vehicle's weight. Realizing that the cargo planes weren't pressurized, as evidenced by the crew's sinus problems, Delbert asked, "Why not get rid of the cargo door?" It was a weighty door, and they had discovered it was easier to leave it open. It was in the way, so Del threw it out, and from then on, they flew their C-47 with an open cargo kick door.

Delbert and his crew usually flew one or two missions per day, but sometimes they worked from pre-dawn past nightfall when they flew the occasional third mission. This was arduous and hazardous work. The weather was the major problem, with heavy rains, ice storms, 70-mile–an-hour winds, and extreme turbulence when flying over the 12,500-foot Naga Hills. Most of their flights took them to 20,000 feet above the Burmese jungles. Occasionally they flew over glacier-covered passes of the Himalayas and into China. This was known as the CBI Hump route. Weather was often treacherous. When the propellers iced over, centrifugal force would eventually fling large chunks of ice off, crashing into the fuselage with a sudden explosion of noise. Whenever the wings became covered in ice, a rubber bladder on the leading edge of each wing was inflated. That caused the ice to crack, and the speed of the C-47 would cause the ice to break free of the craft.

The C-47s were designed for heavy cargo transportation, but they were clumsy, slow, and unarmed. Consequently the C-47s were nicknamed the *Gooney Birds*. Delbert's craft had an even more comical name. The copilot, 2nd Lt. Macabee, had the peculiar habit of going back to the latrine once the craft was in the air. He spent a great deal of time there. He probably had giardiasis, diarrhea, or possibly dysentery, but he did spend most of his time on the toilet. Consequently, 1st Lieutenant Lukaszcyk named his C-47-357 the *Exlax Special*! However, Luke wouldn't allow the name or an icon painted on the nose of the craft. Delbert recalled that "Luke was superstitious about that."

Over the 12-month period that Delbert flew 256 missions in the China-Burma-India Theatre, he transported a large variety of cargo. Usually it was food, supplies, and personnel. Occasionally, though, they did have to transport mules, and cleanup was a dirty, smelly job. They also had to transport Indian rupees and opium bars guarded by the CI (Counter Intelligence) officers. Those peculiar cargo items were used to mollify the Burmese, Naga, Chindit, and Kachin natives of Burma and keep them in the Allied fold. Delbert's crew also evacuated troops out of China over the Himalayas at least twice. When Kweilin Field was about to be overrun by the Japanese, U.S. troops were evacuated by the *Exlax Special*. At Loiwing Factory, where fighter planes were assembled, U.S. civilians and Chinese workers were saved from death by an imminent Japanese incursion when Del and his crew performed another evac mission. Other flights brought K-rations and C-rations to U.S., British, Indian Gurkah, and Chinese troops. Many other cargo items were transported by the *Gooney Birds*, including weapons, ammunition, soap, catsup, Canadian whiskey, toilet paper, Chinese paper money, aluminum irrigation pipes, goats, 55-gallon drums of gasoline, dead soldiers, and badly injured or dying soldiers.

In his later years, Delbert one day revealed, "… I'll never forget those blood-curdling screams that lasted for a half hour before the medic got him enough morphine to reach unconsciousness." He was referring to a pilot who had been downed near Myitkyina. The pilot had been badly burned in the crash, and they were evacuating him to a hospital at Sylhet. Delbert said he didn't want to talk about it as he stared out the window, eyes fixed on Steptoe Butte, but he finally confided, "His whole body was burned. The clothes were burned to his skin. He had no lips, his nose was burned off… no ears… he had no eyelids.... He died before we got to the hospital. We were all sick.... We were white with shock."

Some of the less traumatic but exciting events of high altitude night flying were occurrences of St. Elmo's fire, whereby electrically charged clouds sometimes discharged onto the craft, and balls of fire danced along the wings. At those times, the propellers looked like whirling discs of fire. It was apparently quite a light show. The crew could feel the static electricity on the controls. Delbert said it seemed harmless, but his Squadron members thought it could become hazardous when they were flying fuel cargo, and of course they always had their own fuel tanks. He said they attached several small cords to the trailing edge of the wings. The cords were drenched in oil, and that helped to alleviate the fireworks.

Before one approach to a small landing strip, carved out high in the Naga Hills, one fuel tank ran out and Luke switched over to the backup tank. In the process, the left engine died. As the *Exlax Special* was losing altitude, the pilot got the engine started, but then the right engine went out. They were getting close to the primitive runway and even closer to the jungle canopy. As the plane was hitting the tops of the bamboo, 80 feet above the jungle floor, both engines were finally brought to bear and the steady pilot fought to bring them up over the tree tops and then quickly down onto the runway for a safe, but far from perfect two-point landing.

By early January 1945, the crew of C-47-357 had over 150 flight missions and received promotions. Sgt. Del Gregory had his most dangerous mission on the last flight for the *Exlax Special*. It started out as a routine mission to fly rice and grain out of Dinjan to Myitkyina. But as they approached a mile out from their destination and moved into a low altitude, they started receiving small-arms and machine gun fire from a Japanese patrol. Delbert grabbed an old Springfield rifle and 1st Lt. Macabee pulled his .45 pistol. From the open kick door they fired away at the jungle below, attempting to force the patrol to keep their heads down. However, the C-47 kept receiving heavy fire, much of it around the kick door.

As the *Exlax Special's* crew passed the patrol and arrived at the airfield, they were uncertain of the craft's condition. It was evident that there were numerous bullet holes in the fuselage, but they were unaware that the landing gear had been destroyed. As the craft touched down, it veered to the right and hit three planes. The collisions tore off the craft's right wing and then the plane veered to the left. The left wing was sheared off as it collided with a bulldozer. They kept streaming down the runway without wings, just a fuselage with sparks and fire abounding like some primitive rocket. They finally spun off the runway and collided into a metal storage building. As the dust and smoke settled, Delbert could see that a sharp piece of metal had punctured the fuselage and rested just inches from his head. The men had received some scrapes, but within the hour they were sent back with another damaged but functional C-47. That was the end of the *Exlax Special!* When they received assignment of their next plane, it was agreed that there would be no nickname for this new craft.

After several missions on Luke and Del's new C-47, by mid-January 1945, Delbert had received an informative letter from his mother. Pearl told her son that there was only one number difference in the APO addresses for his letters and those of his childhood friend PFC G. Allen "Al" Latimer. Pearl went on to tell him that Al was stationed at Mohanbari Airfield, and it seemed as if it must be close to Delbert's location, Dinjan Airfield.

Delbert went to his headquarters clerk and discovered that Mohanbari was merely a mile away. Delbert obtained a 2-day pass to visit his friend. It was already a hot, humid morning when Delbert reached Mohanbari, and he promptly visited the field headquarters where he verified Al's barracks location. Al worked in the motor pool, but throughout the previous night he had been loading cargo planes. Del found Al fast asleep in his bunk and chided, "Its reveille, Latimer. Rise and shine!" Al jerked and quickly jumped up, inadvertently ripping his mosquito netting during the commotion. As his eyes cleared, Al yelled "Delbert, you son-of-a-gun!" The two friends lunged toward each other and embraced in a big bear hug.

They tried, but couldn't hold back the tears. Del and Al had enlisted together; then they'd gone through orientation and basic training together, and now, over 2 years later, they met halfway around the world in the middle of a war.

Al got a well-deserved pass, and the two men spent their time reminiscing and touring Dibrugarh, located along the Brahmaputra River. It was the largest local village. They dined in the open-marketplace cafés and perused through the multitude of street peddler wares. Delbert recalled, "We ate a watery curried soup with chicken and noodles, and we drank a refreshment known as *orange squash*, a common Northeast Indian drink of watered-down orange juice mixed with the juice of any number of other available fruits." Delbert also recalled the abundance of Tibetan and Indian Assam peddlers. They lined the streets with blankets upon which they displayed trinkets, Tibetan calendars, and professed health supplements of pulverized musk deer glands and cow bones. Some vendors sold counterfeit coins and fake gemstones. Delbert and Al visited a barber and received a trim and a shoe shine. Their most memorable entertainment was provided by a snake charmer whose defanged, blinded cobra followed the sound of the charmer's gourd flute and moved about, tracing a figure-8 in the air.

Sgt. Del Gregory and PFC Al Latimer had a much needed respite from the turmoil and violence of the war. Their spirits were bolstered by the encounter and they were able to return to their duties with the knowledge that a friend had survived. Shortly after that, Al was transferred; but by war's end, the two young men were back in their small but beloved community of Oakesdale, Washington. But in the meantime, they still had numerous missions to accomplish.

When Delbert thought about the previous May, he recalled the first time he met Luke, his pilot throughout the airlift campaign. Del called him "Sir." 1st Lieutenant Lukaszcyk smiled and replied, "You don't have to be so formal; just call me Luke." For almost a year the two men flew 256 missions together, and they became good friends. Even though Del was an enlisted man and Luke was an officer, Del said Luke treated him as an equal. Each one of their missions had some danger to it, and they grew to depend on each other for their very lives. Usually the problem was the turbulence. For instance, one time going west of the Naga Hills, higher mountains and 70 mph winds created an updraft that threw them into a sudden 500-foot increase in elevation, and just as quickly, they dropped the same distance. Delbert said, "I was thrown to the ceiling, along with the radio and extra boxes of radio tubes. They were all broken, and I was pretty shaken up." Often they were shot at from the ground by Japanese patrols. All the crews feared that they might have to parachute into the Naga Hills. The native Nagas were headhunters; and although some of them helped the Allies, many were unfriendly to any outsiders. All these experiences brought the two men together. Delbert and Luke would have been friends for the rest of their lives. However, the second time they got the chance to go home, Delbert took that opportunity because he was experiencing severe sinus problems, nervousness, and vertigo. Luke chose to stay in theatre for another 6 months, and that was the last time Delbert saw him. While Delbert was convalescing back at Fort George Wright, Spokane, in late March, he got the word about Luke.

Captain John J. Lukaszcyk was serving as co-pilot for Captain Nicholas J. Mandoukos. Mandoukos was referred to as Nick the Greek, and he was considered a hotshot pilot. In other words, he flew like a crazy man. He buzzed elephants, the natives, and their water buffalo within a few feet of the ground. Whenever he received Japanese fire, instead of avoiding it he buzzed the Japanese. He was always trying to fly as close as possible to the trees, and he landed his plane regardless of weather conditions, even in heavy cloud cover. Nobody wanted to fly with him. The hotshot pilot was always ordering enlisted radio operators and lower ranked co-pilots to fly with him when they were done for the day. Everyone, including Delbert, always tried to avoid him. On the night of March 4, 1945, in horrendous weather, Mandoukos crashed his plane on final approach to Ledo, India, killing all 31 passengers and crew, including Luke.

Delbert had lost his best friend from the war years. He lost many other friends and acquaintances while in China, Burma, and India. Another close friend was Claude Adams. Like Delbert, he was a radioman for the 11th. Claude hailed from Danville, Virginia. In October of 1944 Claude's plane disappeared in the jungles of northern Burma, near Naga territory. Neither the plane nor any crew members were ever located. Over 600 planes and 1,000 crewmen were lost on the airlifts. The primary routes of the combat cargo aircraft were referred to as the Skyway to Hell and the Aluminum Trail. Delbert was part of the China-Burma-India Hump, considered the greatest airlift in history, much of it over the highest and most dangerous air routes in all the World War II operations. But by March 15, 1945, Delbert was back home and safe.

Mel's Answer

By December 1942, the youngest brother, Mel, was reluctantly granted permission by Pearl to join the army. At age 17 during his senior year of high school, Army Private Melvin E. Gregory and his best friend, Private Bud "Rabbit" Haire, headed to basic training at Fort Douglas, Utah.

After they finished basic training, and armament and gunnery training, Mel and Bud were temporarily transferred to the Army 10th Mountain Division's Ski Trooper School at Camp Hale, Colorado. Upon successfully finishing the ski training, they were promoted to private first class and transferred to Fort Benning, Georgia, for paratrooper schooling. By January of 1944, PFC Bud Haire was transferred to the Pacific Theatre and PFC Mel Gregory received orders to proceed to North Africa.

Shortly after that, Mel's unit was attached to the 168th Infantry, 34th Infantry Division, and sent to North Africa and then on to Sicily. After additional machine gun training, his unit was sent to mainland Italy. They became part of the assault at Anzio Beach as the initial invasion of the peninsula. The recent arrivals like young Mel were immediately sent to the front lines. Years later, Mel confided that his sergeant had told them that the battlefield at Anzio was utter chaos. The sergeant said he wasn't going to sacrifice the friends he had fought with for over a year in North Africa and Sicily. He went on to tell them that eight of his friends were killed in the first 24 hours upon arrival, and Mel and his unit should keep their damn fool heads down. The Germans had super-howitzer artillery pieces called Big Berthas and Anzio Annies. These Krupp-built, K-5 railway pieces were 218 tons each and fired 350 mm ammunition. The heavy artillery helped the Germans and Italians pin down the American attack force for 4 months, resulting in 5,000 American deaths and 16,000 wounded troops. That was the situation for Mel on April 1, 1944. Vastly outnumbered by German and Italian ground troops and the heavy artillery, Mel and his platoon were sent to the front lines into a situation that was akin to suicide. Against overwhelming odds and the heaviest of fighting, they held the enemy back for 7 days.

Mel was fighting from a machine gun nest on a ridge above the beachhead. There were six other infantrymen in his squad. Suddenly a German grenade was launched into his nest. He remembers a deafening explosion, and Mel was momentarily knocked unconscious. Shrapnel hit Mel in the left side of his face, arm, and leg. When he awoke, the bleeding had subsided, but he couldn't open his left eye and he was experiencing severe pain. The other six members of his squad were either dead or unconscious. Before he could determine their condition, a dozen Germans overran the nest and slit the throats of his fellow squad members. Since he was conscious, Mel was taken prisoner, and he was ruthlessly handled.

Mel found himself among about 50 prisoners in an open field and guarded by a dozen German soldiers. During the first night he slipped away. After running for a mile, maybe more, he stumbled onto another escaped American prisoner of war. The two of them analyzed their predicament and decided to travel together by night and attempt to find a stand of trees or a grove in which to hide during the day. Before daybreak they found just such a grove of olive trees and fell asleep there. They were awakened by an Italian farmer. Fortunately, this farmer detested the Germans. The farmer led Mel and his fellow escapee to his farm house. His wife prepared a meal for the young Americans and then he took them to his barn. He said they could hide there as long as they needed. However, 3 days later a German patrol came to the farmer's door. The menacing officer in charge had a long discussion with the farmer. Mel and his companion could see the Nazi officer lecturing to the old man. The old farmer seemed to be sweating profusely, and Mel could see his legs shaking. Within moments the officer had his patrol enter the barn and take Mel and his friend. They were not harmed but were marched a great distance where they waited in another open field. Eventually, other prisoners were brought to this staging area, and the total group was taken by train in crowded boxcars to an area outside of annexed Vienna, Austria. From there they were force marched to Stalag 7A in Germany. Mel recalled that a few prisoners tried to run from the march, but they were shot in the back.

Mel spent over 13 months in stalags as they were moved from one to another to keep them away from the Russian front lines. Much of the imprisonment took place in Stalag 7A. It was here where photos were taken of the prisoners. Unlike his oldest brother Charles, Mel did receive some medical treatment, Red Cross packages, regular meals, and letters from his mother. Unfortunately, no surgery was offered for Mel's combat wounds. Without receiving the needed surgical treatment, Mel eventually lost the sight in his left eye.

Mel attempted another escape on his own. He headed east, away from the center of the German forces and toward the Russian held area in Poland. He hid in brushy areas during the day and traveled by night. However, he was captured again and temporarily imprisoned in German-occupied Poland at Stalag 2B. Mel was again force-marched back to Germany.

Over the next 10 months Mel was transferred back and forth to several stalags, depending on where the Russians were applying the most pressure. At one point he was housed in a railroad car for 11 days with very little food or water. Some of the prison camps where he was housed included stalags 7A, 2B, 3B, and 3C. Locations of the prison camps were near Moosburg, Luckenwald, Hammerstein/ Schlochau, Wellstein, Alt Drewitz bei Kustrin, and Furstenberg. While Mel was at Luckenwald, he contracted scarlet fever and was hospitalized during August and September.

When he was returned to the prisoner of war camp, Mel was placed on work details. Some of the work was construction, but much of it was farm labor. Although the Germans fed their prisoners better than did the Japanese, it was still very short of a light diet. When Mel was captured on April 7, 1944, he weighed 155 pounds; within the year, he had fallen to 115 pounds.

While Mel was at Moosburg Stalag 7A, he thought he saw a familiar face staring at him, but he was unsure. After a while the American prisoner came up to Mel and asked if he remembered him. It was Fred Schuman, a young man from Garfield, Washington. Mel and Fred were at the same grade level in school. They grew up merely 10 miles apart. They had played against each other in basketball since junior high, and they played across the line from each other in high school football. The two prisoners of war had many friends and acquaintances in common. They became fast friends, shared their war experiences with each other, and reminisced about the good old days, growing up in Whitman County. Mel learned that Fred had been wounded three times, the first being in the Battle of the Bulge on December 16, 1944.

While a prisoner of the Nazis, Mel was allowed to keep a scrapbook. He wrote a few comments in the book. Remarkably, he was able to sketch a number of drawings of guards and fellow prisoners. Mel also passed the book around, and other prisoners added comments and sketches. Some of his favorite additions were the labels from a few of their Red Cross canned goods. Mel said that the scrapbook always gave him hope. He cherished that book and kept it close by the rest of his life.

Mel also cherished the letters from his mother. And he was allowed to send an occasional letter, usually on some scrap of paper. The following letter wasn't dated:

Dear Mom,

I would have written sooner, but this is the first chance I've had to write. I know you have worried lot about me. I'm O.K. and being treated alright. Tell the kids hello for me. I've wondered if you ever got the money I sent home. Send me some chocolate fudge and cigarettes when you get the opportunity. We get some in our Red Cross packages, but not quite enough.

We work part of the time and also have plenty of time to play ball, so it makes the time pass faster. Have you heard from Charlie lately? I hope so.

I would have sent you something for your birthday and Mother's day, but I just couldn't. I'll make up for it on the next one. There isn't much to write about. Don't forget to send the chocolate, all you can. I'll be able to write every week from now on.

Love, Mel

Years later, Delbert commented on that letter. He said that Pearl did get the money Mel had sent her. It was the $700 that Mel had won in poker games played aboard the troop ship that transported Mel to the European Theatre. Mel proved to be an outstanding judge of character, and he could easily read the nervous faces of his fellow G.I.s. His $700 winnings was a substantial amount of money in 1944, probably about a half year's wages for the average job. Pearl put it in Mel's bank account so that it was there for Mel when he got home. Also, concerning that letter, it was interesting that Mel asked for the same thing that Charles had requested 3 years earlier— chocolate fudge. Apparently Pearl had that recipe perfected, because it was a popular item at the IGA confectionary as well.

Mel survived his experiences with the Nazis. About 14 months after he had entered the European Theatre, PFC Melvin E. Gregory was liberated by Russian troops on May 4, 1945. Upon liberation, the freed American prisoners of war were allowed to stay with the Russians or go off on their own. The Russians didn't show much interest in the welfare of the freed troops. Also the care of the prisoners was apparently overlooked by their Nazi captors during those last few weeks of heavy fighting between the Germans and the Russians.

Mel and his fellow prisoners were hungry, but they chose to stay with the Russians for two weeks. However, the Russians, short on rations, wouldn't share food with the liberated prisoners. The Red Army was promised $50 per American prisoner repatriated, but apparently that wasn't sufficient reward for the Russians to take care of the Americans. Consequently, the Americans had to find their own food. Mel and his friends raided several abandoned markets for minimal sustenance, but one day they noticed a healthy looking cow in a nearby field. The hungry Americans slaughtered and butchered the cow. They built a large fire and scavenged some tomato paste, pepper, beer, brown sugar, kettles, and paint brushes. They made their own sauce, and the hungry young soldiers patiently waited for their barbequed beef — Texas style!

As the Americans accompanied the Russian troops to the west, Mel became suspicious of the Russians' behavior. He felt they were acting like anything but friendly allies. They often pushed the Americans, and they were becoming belligerent. Some of the Red Army troops pointed their rifles at the Americans, dry fired, and laughed uproariously. When a Red soldier pointed his rifle at Mel, he tore into the Russian. A dozen other Red troopers beat and kicked Mel, but he got loose and knocked several to the ground. Mel had enough of the haughty Russians. He left them and commandeered a motorcycle. The young soldier headed west, where he eventually spotted American G.I.s. Finally, the youngest of the brothers was on his way back home.

Mel discovered that he hadn't lost his touch at games of chance; on the troop ship back to the states, he parlayed some more funds at the poker table. Mel, infused with cash, was transferred to Camp Beale, California. When he arrived, he was able to go back to

Oakesdale on leave, where he met with a relieved Pearl, Speck, and Delbert. When he returned to Camp Beale, Mel was awarded the Combat Infantry Badge and the Purple Heart. The youngest of the brothers was finally separated from service on October 27, 1945, and headed back to Oakesdale. After he had been in the fight of his life — for his life — Mel had survived.

TSgt. Donald Gregory,
Marrakesh, Morocco, 1943.

Cpl. Delbert Gregory, Kirtland Field,
New Mexico, 1944.

TSgt. Don "Speck" Gregory's crashed B-17, *Stardust*, 347th Squadron,
99th Bomb Group, Algiers, Algeria, 1943. *USAF Archives*

Cpl. Del Gregory's C-47, *Exlax Special,* 11th Combat Cargo
Squadron, 3rd Combat Cargo Group, pre-crash,
Myitkyina, Burma, 1944.

Pvt. Mel Gregory, Camp Hale,
Colorado, 1943

Sgt. Delbert Gregory,
Calcutta, India, 1945

Sgt. Del Gregory,
Dinjan Airfield, India, 1945.

PFC Al Latimer
Mohanbari Airfield, India, 1945.

Sgt. Del Gregory awarded Distinguished Flying Cross,
Ft. George Wright, WA, 1945. *USAF Archives*

Mel and Speck, Oakesdale, 1942.

Bud Haire and Mel, Camp Hale (ski school), 1943.

Bud Haire and Mel Gregory, on leave, Oakesdale, 1944.

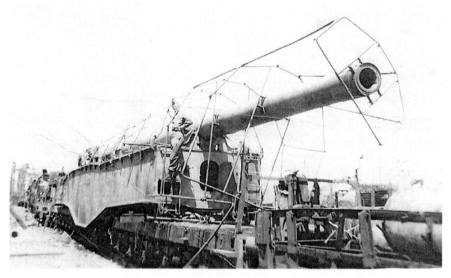

Germany's "Anzio Annie," Krupp's K-5, 218 ton, 350 mm Railway Howitzer, Anzio, Italy, 1944.

PFC Mel Gregory,
Ft. Benning,
Georgia, 1944.

Mel's POW photo,
Stalag 7A, Germany,
1944.

PFC Mel Gregory
with Purple Heart,
1945.

A sketch of Mel from a fellow POW at Stalag 7A, Germany, 1944.

Nina Lee Littleton, High
School Graduation, 1942.

Nina and Jean, Spokane
Trade School, 1943.

Nina Littleton's ID badge,
SPAAD, 1944.

SPAAD, Hornet R-1690.
USAF Archives

Chapter 10

The Heart in Too Many Pieces

*The best and most beautiful things in the world cannot be seen,
nor touched, but are felt in the heart.*

— Helen Keller

By July 1942, Charles and Ernest were transferred from Camp O'Donnell to Cabanatuan Camp #1. After months of sickness, dysentery, and deaths, Camp O'Donnell was referred to as a benjo (Japanese word for toilet). The ground was densely covered everywhere in crusted and wet mucous, defecation, regurgitation, and blood. There was no pretense of sanitation. By the end of June 1942, over 1,500 Americans and over 20,000 Filipinos had died in Camp O'Donnell—in just three months. Camp #1 wasn't much better, but it was a little more sanitary. Charles had been experiencing recurring bouts of malaria, dysentery, and beriberi, a result of malnourishment, and he had dropped to under 100 pounds. Ernest and Charles did take some comfort in that their old squad mates Nels and Fran were still alive at the new camp.

There was easier access to water at Cabanatuan, and the troops were allowed to cook their own food. Usually, a truck would dump filthy, rotted, bug-infested rice on the ground and the Americans would cook that in a kawa or large cast-iron pot to make a watery porridge. Also, the troops were able to set up a makeshift hospital, but it was frustrating for the medics because there was little medication or medical equipment, and most of the hospital staff members were equally sick or diseased. The camp prisoners were given a typewriter and postcards. Prisoners queued up for hours to send a card, as a few healthy soldiers took turns typing. However, only a small amount of information was allowed, and it had to be approved by the camp censor. Charles's first communication since December 1941 was typed up in September of 1942 but wasn't received until March 1943. It gave the following scant and inaccurate information, mostly in form:

IMPERIAL JAPANESE ARMY

I am interned at 'The Philippine Military Prison Camp #1.'
My health is 'fair.'
I am 'well.'
(Re: Family); 'Don't worry.'
Please give my best regards to 'all the family and friends.'

Charles's health was not "fair," nor was he "well." He was very ill, but Charles was fortunate to have his old friends Fran and Nels and his lifelong friend Ernest Harold Loy helping to feed him as they in turn watched out for each other. Without each other's help and attention, they would probably have died by the end of 1942.

Eventually, Charles was in better health at Cabanatuan Camp #1 than he had been upon arrival. Although he was still suffering from bouts of malaria and dysentery, Charles had survived a near-death run-in with beriberi. He was fortunate that it was dry beriberi, which gave him tremors, high fever, digestive problems, and numbness in his limbs. On the other hand, some prisoners contracted wet beriberi, which caused tremendous swelling of the entire body and many open, seeping sores, and almost always led to death. One disgusting aspect of wet beriberi was the seeping sores. If a soldier sat for very long, when he stood, liquid would pour out of each fetid opening. Other than that, the only other problems were flies, fleas, ticks, crabs, maggots, bedbugs, and lice.

Between March 1943 and March 1944, Pearl received three more postcards from Charles and the Imperial Japanese Army. In them, Charles's health was described as either good or fair. They stated that he was well and not under treatment. He asked to say "hello" to his longtime friend Laverne Marple. Additionally, he hoped all his friends and family were well and that he hoped to be home soon.

By this time, Pearl was suffering and in tears almost daily. She had been learning about the Japanese treatment of prisoners. She had two sons in aerial combat and her youngest son was an injured prisoner of the Nazis. She certainly felt that things couldn't have been much worse, and her dreams of having six college-educated children were in the distant past. Now she only hoped and prayed for their survival.

Charles's friends had been sent to Las Piñas Prison Camp, and he missed them. Although he had survived the beriberi, Charles was still malnourished and vastly underweight. However, he was better off than many of the prisoners in Cabanatuan, so in January 1944 Charles was sent to a labor-camp prison—Lipa Batangas Camp #10B. Upon arrival he was allowed to send one last postcard, but it wasn't received until over a year later, on February 5, 1945. Remarkably optimistic, addressed to his mother, Charles stated, "I am still well and uninjured, I hope everyone at home is the same. We are expecting mail in the near future. Best regards to all and tell Laverne to leave a few pheasants and fish for me when I return." It was signed "Love, Charles R. Gregory." Once again, he was neither well nor uninjured. He never received any mail; and, sadly, Charles would not return with his friends to his beloved fishing.

Charles didn't know that being sent to Lipa was almost like receiving a death sentence, or at least the prelude to one. At Lipa, Charles was forced to do hard labor for 10 hours a day, building a runway for the Japanese air force. He was beaten daily by a brutally sadistic cadre of guards. After a short time, the guards cut the already meager rations to a bare minimum because work was not proceeding as fast as they demanded. Rations were never increased after the cut.

In late 1944, the Americans were finally making progress toward the Philippines, so prisoners of war were being sent to Japan.

Charles's friend Francis Agnes had already been transported to Japan on the hellship *Coral Maru;* and several months prior to that, Charles's old friend from Oakesdale, Jack Elkins, was sent to a labor camp in Yokohama, Japan, aboard a hellship he called the *Haro Maru.* But in September, Charles, battered, malnourished, and barely alive, was temporarily sent to Bilibid Prison Camp as a staging area. And on October 1, Charles and approximately 1,100 other prisoners from various camps were sent to Pier 7, Manila, and herded aboard the *Hokusen Maru,* captained by the inhumane Tomiichi Tsutsui. Like many of the other ships in harbor, red crosses clearly adorned the smoke stack to keep the ship from being bombed during its shipments for the Imperial Army. However, in yet another direct violation of the Geneva Convention, international law, and basic humanity, the Imperial Captain Tsutsui ordered that the crosses be painted out, since the ship was carrying American prisoners.

The temperature was reaching record heights at this time. The modest looking ship's lower hulls reached temperatures in excess of 115 degrees during the day. The hull was divided into two sections, each about 50 feet square and each holding over 500 men barely able to move. Forced onto a ladder, Charles descended into the shadowy darkness of the bow hull with his longtime friends Nels and Ernie nearby. The aft hull was putrid from carrying livestock, but the bow hull had carried coal. The floor was littered in coal dust and covered with sharp pieces of coal throughout. Every time someone moved, black powdery dust filled the stuffy, hot air. As prisoners moved, they couldn't help cutting themselves on the shards of coal.

Charles was estimated to be down to about 70 pounds at this point—skin draped on skeleton—legs and buttocks painfully raw with rashes and open sores. Lipa Batangas Camp had been extremely hard on him. Like so many of the men, he had a recurring bout of malaria.

Most of the men had dysentery and couldn't control their eliminations. By the time the ship left harbor on October 3, the hull was a dark, suffocating, dusty, fetid, hellish pit. The men had buckets lowered to them in which they could eliminate. The buckets were raised, dumped overboard, rinsed in the sea water, brought up, and filled with stale water from which the men could drink. The men were lowered rice in the same buckets that had previously carried their watery feces. The men labored to breathe, and they could taste a putrid stench in their mouths. The conditions were beyond belief. In their hallucinations from disease, some men thought they were dead and in hell. Therefore these transports were called hellships.

Nels told Pearl that during Charles's last 2 days he couldn't eat or drink. Ernest and Nels tried to feed him, but Charles said he was going to die and they should take his ration. In later years, Francis Agnes said that at night he could still hear the cries and moans of his fellow prisoners on his own hellship, the *Coral Maru* – it was nightmarish. In later years, Ernest's children said he suffered terrible nightmares. They said that each night they were awakened by their dad's violently visceral screaming. Like Fran, he too was returning to his hellship every night in his horrible dreams. The young men's experiences with the Battle of Bataan, the Bataan Death March, and 2½ years in prison camps had been bad enough. But the hellship nightmare was unimaginably horrific.

Neither the prisoners nor the guards knew the actual name of the *Hokusen Maru*. The guards called it the *Haro Maru* (floating ship). The prisoners with any sense of humor left in them sardonically referred to the hellship as the *Haro Benjo* (floating toilet).

Shortly after the ship left harbor in a convoy, it was attacked by U.S. submarines. Some ships in the convoy were destroyed with all prisoners aboard. However, the *Hokusen Maru*, though battered, was unharmed. On the morning of October 5, a rope was lowered into the hull to tie the lifeless body of Cpl. William "Bill" Bowra. A couple of his friends were allowed to climb up and lower him into the sea with a few words. The friends were then hit with sticks and forced back down into the sweltering, putrid abyss. The next morning found Capt. Howard Sabin and SSgt. Norman Thenell also released from the pain and nightmare. Over the next five days, 16 more ropes were lowered for bodies. As the *Hokusen Maru* harbored in Hong Kong Bay at daybreak on October 11, the convoy was attacked by American bombers, but Charles's ship was once again unharmed.

However, the prisoners were thrown from side to side and banged into walls and each other as the attacks took place. Then after the prisoners sat for 24 hours in smothering heat, eight more ropes were lowered into the holds of the *Hokusen Maru*. In the early morning of October 12, 1944, those ropes carried up the lifeless bodies of PFC Henry Cichocki, Sgt. Richard Clarke, PFC Carl Deemer, Pvt. Floyd Garland, PFC John Laurence, Midshipman Leo Olen, Cpl. Frank Sanchez, and finally Air Corpsman Private Charles R. Gregory, Jr. It was the ship's deadliest day. Nelson Quast and Ernest Loy came up the ladder and lowered Charles into his watery grave. Ernie said, "Rest in peace, my friend." and Nels yelled, "Death, where's your sting now!" He was probably remembering part of Alexander Pope's poem, partially taken from Corinthians:

> *The World recedes, it disappears,*
> *Heaven opens on my eyes, my ears*
> *With sounds seraphic ring;*
> *Lend, lend your wings! I mount! I fly!*
> *O grave! Where is thy victory?*
> *Oh death! Where is thy sting?*

Charles's death was a passing away of a life, but it was also the passing away of unbearable pain, agony, and incredible suffering. Between October 5 and October 29, 36 troops died aboard the *Hokusen Maru*—one British soldier and 35 Americans.

Over a year later, Ernest told Pearl that when he saw Charles boarding the ship he almost didn't recognize him. Ernest and Nelson had spent the previous few months at Las Piñas Prison Camp, where conditions had been somewhat better than at Cabanatuan #1. However, Charles had been at Lipa, one of the most pernicious work camps of World War II. The Lipa prisoners were provided starvation rations, and they were overworked and beaten daily. Ernest said his old friend appeared to be in the worst condition possible.

His skin was simply hanging on his bones. He weighed perhaps 70 pounds. His body was covered with open sores, rashes, raw patches of skin, red welts, and broken blood blisters.

By the time Charles's friends visited Pearl to inform her of his last years and moments, Charles had been dead for 13 months. The angst-ridden mother had received her last communication from Charles 10 months earlier. It had been written almost 2 years previous to that. Pearl didn't break down. Beginning with the death of her first born infant Neva, Pearl had been hardened to tragedy long before. She had been waiting for word from Charles, worrying day by day, for such a long time. She had hope, but she was realistic.

Pearl was buoyed to some extent by the fact that three of her sons had returned from the war; it brought her joy to see the three soldiers together. But the news of Charles's death stung deeply and was yet another reason for her shattered heart. She could hardly talk over the next few months. Within a few days of the boys' visits, she received her first official notice. A telegram arrived in late November from H. N. Gilbert Acting Adjutant General of the Army. It pounded the ache further into her heart. A few days later she received this letter from Major General Edward F. Witsell:

> *It is with profound regret that I confirm the recent telegram informing you of the death of your son, Staff Sergeant Charles R. Gregory, 19,032,202, Air Corps, who was previously reported a prisoner of war.*
>
> *An official message has now been received which states that he died on 12 October 1944 as a result of malaria while aboard a ship en route to Japan. He was buried at sea in Hong Kong Bay.*
>
> *I realize the great suspense you have endured during this unfortunately long period and now, the finality to those hopes which you have cherished for his safety. Although little may be said or done at this time to alleviate your grief, it is my fervent hope that later the knowledge that he gave his life for his country may be of sustaining comfort to you.*
>
> *I extend my profound sympathy in your bereavement.*

A few weeks later she received a letter addressed 10 December 1945 from Colonel Charles A. Piddock, Air Corps, Deputy for Personnel, Headquarters, Spokane Air Technical Service Command. It stated, "It was with deep regret that this Command received official notification of the death of your son... I express my own personal sympathy in your loss." It further stated that Staff Sergeant Charles R. Gregory had been promoted four grades for valiant time in service and that Pearl may be entitled to "gratuity pay, arrears in pay, pension, U.S. Government Life Insurance, Commercial Life Insurance, and Social Security Benefits."

Each notification seemed to hurt more than the next. By this time, in addition to the emotional toll, Pearl was also experiencing severe physical pain internally. She received another letter that had been typed on the 1st of January, 1946. Almost sounding as if it were from royalty, this letter was addressed from the Office of the Commander-in-Chief of the United States Army Forces in the Pacific. It was from none other than Dugout Doug! Of course, being the ever self-promoting politician, interspersed among his expressions of sympathy, there were references of his famous return to the Philippines. And since he was obviously too busy to sign the expression of grief, the letter bore a stamped signature.

A few months later, Pearl visited a doctor in Spokane. He performed some tests and asked her to return for additional tests and evaluation. Eventually, she was informed that she had cancer and it had spread throughout her body.

During Pearl's last few months she tried to reach out and extract at least some financial remuneration from the people responsible for her eldest son's suffering and death. She obtained written letters from Charles's friends. They were with him much of the time from entrance into the service throughout the death march and much of the imprisonment. Those letters told the whole story of his mistreatment. Pearl hired Don Burcham, an attorney, to present her case to the War Department, Office of the Judge Advocate General, Claims, and Litigation Group. She sent copies of the letters from Ernest Loy and Nelson Quast, along with an affidavit summarizing the treatment of her son. She received the following letter from the War Department, Office of the Judge Advocate General, Washington 25, District of Columbia:

JAGD/D-258247 (Gregory, Pearl)

13 Nov 1946

Mrs. Pearl Gregory
Oakesdale, Washington

Dear Madam:

Receipt is acknowledged of your letter of 21 October 1946, together with sworn affidavit in your claim against the Japanese Government for the death of your son aboard a prison ship.

In accordance with previous communication of this office dated 14 August 1946, all correspondence and related papers are this date being referred to the Department of State for further consideration by that department.

Sincerely yours,

Claude E. Fernandez
Lieutenant Colonel, JAGD
Assistant Chief
Claims and Litigation Group

Outstanding; her claim was being forwarded to the diplomatic corps—people who could use a thousand words to say nothing. In other words, her claim would be buried. Finally, she was informed that the U.S. Federal Government couldn't sue the Japanese Government. President Truman had agreed to that stipulation as part of the Japanese surrender. Apparently, it was not the unconditional surrender promised by both Roosevelt and Truman. Pearl had been a proud supporter of the two Democrat presidents in the past. But now she put politicians in a category she had previously reserved for insurance men, greedy bankers, and MacArthur—untrustworthy, self-promoting, and self-serving.

Pearl was not alone in her latent disdain for Roosevelt and especially MacArthur. Ernest Loy's children shared that although Ernest had learned to forgive the Japanese people as a race, he always held a deep hatred of MacArthur. Ernest felt that the politically oriented general's incompetence, misunderstanding, and short sightedness were compounded by his cowardice evidenced by the abandonment of thousands of American troops.

Nevertheless, Pearl had to bear the pain of her son's torture, starvation, mistreatment, and death. That's how she spent the final month of her life. As weeks went on and her days became short, Pearl became delirious. She often had conversations as if she were talking to Charles, sometimes the elder, sometimes the younger, but it was usually hard to discern which. Pearl was comforted by her children. Delbert and Chet and their wives Nina and Millie were in Oakesdale. Mel arrived from nearby Cheney, where he was attending Eastern Washington State College. Nita arrived from Seattle, and Speck flew in from Ft. Worth, Texas. They stayed with her continuously for 48 hours as she faded and became more delirious. Early in the afternoon of December 24, 1946, the siblings caravanned with Pearl to Deaconess Hospital in Spokane. Their mother lapsed into a coma before nightfall and died on Christmas Eve... Pearl's long struggle was over. Funeral services were held at 11:00 a.m. on Friday, December 27, 1946, at the Oakesdale Community Presbyterian Church. Later that day she was laid to rest with her husband in the Winona Community Cemetery.

Del, Speck, and Mel, who each narrowly survived
World War II; Oakesdale, Washington, 1945.

Gpaw Charles
sister Pearl

Pearl still hoped for Charles's
return; Oakesdale, 1945.

From:
Name
Charles R. Gregory
Charles R. Gregory

Nationality AMERICAN

Rank Private

Camp PHILIPPINE MILITARY
      PRISON CAMP 1

To: Mrs. Pearl Gregory
     Oakesdale, Washington
     U. S. A.

IMPERIAL JAPANESE ARMY

1. I am interned at the Philippine Military Prison Camp #1

2. My health is — excellent; good; fair; poor.

3. I am — injured; sick in hospital; under treatment; not under treatment.

4. I am — improving; not improving; better; well.

5. Please see that don't worry
   is taken care of.

6. (Re: Family): Hope to be home soon.

7. Please give my best regards to family and friends.

Front and back of the last postcard Charles was able to send
from Cabanatuan Prison Camp #1. He was not allowed
to provide accurate information; sent December 1942,
it was received a year later.

北　鮮　丸

Pvt. Charles R. Gregory, Jr. died aboard the *Hokusen Maru*
on October 12, 1944. Boarded on October 1, 36 POWs
died between October 5th and 29th. They were buried
at sea by their friends. *National Archives*

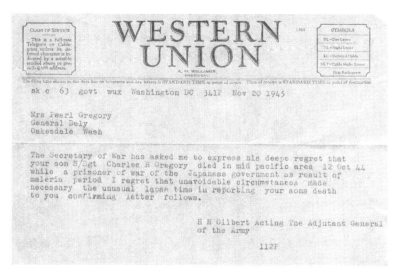

Pearl received official notice of her son's death in late 1945,
13 months after the fact. She was also visited by Ernest Loy
and Nelson Quast, who told her of Charles's last years
and moments.

Pearl and TSgt. Don Gregory, Oakesdale,
1946, humbled by the news of Charles's
death and Pearl's cancer.

Chapter 11

Picking Up the Pieces

Life is a blend of laughter and tears, a combination of rain and sunshine.

— Norman Vincent Peale

Chester Earl, Pearl's middle son, was the first of the brothers to marry. On November 23, 1941, he wedded Mildred Lee, his childhood sweetheart. She came to Seattle to live with Chet while he was working for Boeing. Over the next 3 years they had two sons. In late 1945, as Boeing was starting to downsize, Chet and Millie returned to Oakesdale to be closer to Pearl. They worked for Bob Lee, Millie's father, at the IGA grocery, as well as Bob's Kozy Inn and Restaurant. Millie also assisted Pearl with her bakery and confectionery in the IGA store.

It was a great comfort to Pearl to have Chet and Millie so close during her final year. After Pearl's death, Chet obtained a position with Hills Bros. Coffee and was assigned a sales route in the Walla Walla, Washington, area. They moved to Walla Walla and continued to live there until Chet's promotion and reassignment to the Seattle area in 1968. After a decade there, Chet retired, but still continued to do small construction and home remodeling jobs.

Chet was active in auctions throughout Washington and the Pacific Northwest. Millie was always proud of her fine furniture, household appliances, and automobiles that Chet obtained through shrewd auction deals. Chet contributed service to his community through the Benevolent and Protective Order of Elks. He was an active member for over 40 years and spent much of his extra time raising money for needy children.

In 1992 Chet developed cancer, and by the time he went to a doctor, the disease had metastasized throughout much of his body. He had no intention of facing and fighting his final battle. However, he prepared for the end. Chet sold their large home and purchased a smaller single-level home for Millie. He put all their financial affairs in order so that Millie would be provided for during her final years. Chet was a good man, but he preferred not to fight. When everything was in order on July 4, 1992, Chet took a hose to the closed garage and, like he had always done as a child, sadly, he ran from his last battle.

Donald "Speck" Gregory was the next of Pearl's children to wed. Ruth did wait for Speck to return from overseas. After Speck had finished his tour at Gowen Air Base, he was scheduled to be transferred to Ellsworth Air Base, Rapid City, South Dakota to train flight recruits. He had a short leave first and returned home to his mother and the girl who said she would wait. Ruth and Speck agreed to marry on December 1, 1943, and they proceeded on their adventure to South Dakota.

After Speck completed his contracted time with the Army Air Corps, he returned to Oakesdale with Ruth and a daughter. Speck attended a one-year mechanical engineering technology program at Gonzaga University. When finished he reenlisted in the Air Force at his old rank of Technical Sergeant and was stationed with Carswell Air Force Base, Flight Training School near Fort Worth, Texas. Over the next few years Speck and Ruth had two more daughters and a son. But in 1957 Ruth was stricken with kidney disease and passed away.

Speck requested and received a transfer to Fairchild Air Force Base near Spokane. He took his four children to live in Oakesdale with Ruth's parents, and he visited them at every opportunity. Speck also spent time fishing with his brother Delbert, as well as the old family friend, Jack Elkins. Eventually Speck met and married Virginia Kent Bruihl. Virginia had three daughters from her previous marriage. Speck and Virginia bought a home in Spokane and raised their seven children there. Jack Elkins and his wife, Maravene Trimble Elkins, had many dinner parties with Speck and Virginia. It was at this time that Virginia and Speck realized the connections they had with each other as well as their friends, the Elkinses.

Virginia thought Speck had always lived in Oakesdale. When Speck was reminiscing with Jack, Virginia discovered that Speck's early years were at the farm west of Winona. Virginia shared that she was raised at a farm east of Benge. The couple stumbled upon the fact that they spent their early years growing up only a few miles from each other, and their parents had attended the same square dances, one of which was at the old Gregory homestead. Furthermore, Virginia discovered that her brother, Herb Kent, was Jack's closest friend in the Japanese Prison Camp. They had worked on the same details near Yokohama and bunked next to each other for 2 years. Jack shared, "We used to sabotage the Jap ships we were forced to build. Herb and I used to loosen the rivets and put sand in the grease buckets and propellers." Jack had also visited Speck's brother, Charles, when they were both stationed near Manila before the bombing started. The world seemed to have some order to it.

Speck was a member of the Optimist International service club and spent much of his extra time raising funds for needy children. He also spent a good deal of his time hunting and fishing with his brother Delbert. One of his proudest days came in 2008, when he brought his 11-year-old great-grandson, Tyler, to Oakesdale. Delbert had brought his 9-year-old great-grandson, Trenton. The four of them traveled the 10 miles southeast to Garfield Pond, a small lake reserved for juveniles (15 and under). The old men helped their progeny fish and encouraged them. Sometimes they took the boys' rods and reels and showed them the correct techniques. After the boys had each caught a few fish, the octogenarians discovered that they were doing the fishing. The young boys were off attempting to catch frogs, turtles, and crawdads, much like Speck and Delbert had done at Rock Creek near the homestead, some 80 years earlier. The family had come full circle! Both boys were there at the Oakesdale Cemetery on September 19, 2009, when retired Master Sergeant Donald F. Gregory was laid to rest in the military section.

The next of Pearl's children to marry was Delbert Eugene. He wedded Nina Lee Littleton, his childhood sweetheart. While Del was in the service, Nina took the Airplane Engine Assembly and Repair mechanic course at Spokane Trade School. Upon completing the course, she used those skills to work for the Spokane Army Air Depot at Galena Field (Fairchild AFB). She became a genuine "Rosie the Riveter" for over 2 years as Nina and Del exchanged love letters and betrothed. On Easter Sunday, 1945, they were married at the home of Nina's Aunt Edna and Uncle Robert Crow. Easter landed on April 1st that year. In later years, a great deal of playful humor was heaped upon the couple for marrying on April Fools' Day. The following article appeared in the April 6, 1945, *Oakesdale Weekly Reminder*, No. 90, published by the Alpha Study Club:

> *Easter Sunday evening at 8 p.m. in the presence of about seventy relatives and friends Sgt. Delbert Gregory and Nina L. Littleton were united in marriage by the Rev. Gerald Manley. The candlelight service took place in the home of Mr. and Mrs. Robert Crow with candelabras and baskets of spring flowers serving as a beautiful setting for the double ring ceremony.*
>
> *The bride, a popular Oakesdale girl, who for the past two years has been in Spokane, was very charming in a gray cardigan suit with blue accessories and a talisman rose bud corsage.*
>
> *Miss Betty Warner sang 'Always' accompanied at the piano by Ruth Littleton, the bride's sister, who also played the wedding march.*

The groom, who has just recently returned from active overseas duty, was attended by his brother, Chester Gregory, of Seattle.

The bride's mother, Mrs. Sam Littleton, wore a dress of black crepe and a corsage of gardenias. Mrs. Pearl Gregory, the groom's mother, wore a powder blue dress with a gardenia corsage.

Mrs. Lloyd Elkins Best served the very beautiful wedding cake and Miss Shirley Kendall poured. Assisting at the refreshment table were Mrs. Charlie Crow, Mrs. Roy Hall, Mrs. Chester Gregory, Miss Jannie Crow, and Miss Jo Anne Crow.

After a brief honeymoon the young couple will go to Santa Monica, California, where Sgt. Gregory will await further orders. The many friends of the couple wish for them every success and happiness upon the sea of matrimony and hope for a soon ending of the present conflict so they might enjoy to the fullest their new venture in life. Congratulations, Delbert and Nina, from all!

After they returned, Delbert worked as maintenance man and custodian for the Oakesdale School District for 37 years. Nina and Delbert had three children and, when the youngest started school, Nina began working as a school bus driver and the assistant custodian; she continued for 26 years.

Delbert was an Honorary Chapter Farmer for the Oakesdale Future Farmers of America. He was also a president of the Oakesdale Parent-Teachers Association. Delbert hunted deer with his old high school buddy Stanley "Sammy" Henrickson. He hunted pheasants throughout much of northern Whitman County with his brother Speck. They fished for steelhead in the Snake River, trout in Rock, Amber, Clear, Badger, Williams, and Waitts lakes, and small-mouth bass in South Twin Lake, Washington, Upper Twin and Lower Twin lakes, Idaho, and an upstream slough of a secret tributary of the Pend Oreille River where Speck and Del caught 10- and 9-pound small-mouth bass, respectively.

In 1988, Delbert, Nina, and a few friends established the McCoy Valley Museum in honor of Oakesdale's centennial. Both Delbert and Nina served as president of the museum board several times each, and at 90 and 89 they still participated in fundraisers for the museum.

During the 1980s and '90s, Delbert and Nina traveled around the nation to attend several China-Burma-India Hump Pilots Association Reunions. Delbert also spent several years sharing his World War II experiences at Oakesdale High School Veterans Day ceremonies. In October of 2010, Delbert was proud to participate in the National Honor Flight. Along with 30 other World War II veterans from the Inland Northwest, Delbert flew to Washington, DC, to view the World War II Memorial and participate in a number of guided tours of the capital city. Delbert and Nina still live in Oakesdale, Washington, and during the writing of this book they have turned 90 and 89, respectively.

The next of Pearl's children to marry was Nita. Nita had a short marriage to Ray Miller that ended after less than 2 years. Three years after that marriage ended, Nita met a young sailor, and the two of them were enamored with each other. On May 1, 1945, Juanita Arline married Howard Vernon Long. After World War II, Howard was employed as a lumberjack near Roseburg, Oregon. Howard never conjured up the image of the standard lumberjack. Indeed, anyone who ever spent time with him felt he fit the image of a college professor. Howard was extremely well-read. He was an enthralling conversationalist and he had myriad facts, figures, and anecdotes at his disposal. He was also a proven fly tyer, fisherman, and hunter. Over the course of their marriage, the couple moved back and forth several times from Roseburg, Oregon, northern California, and Wrangell Island, Alaska, depending on where the work was available.

Nita and Howard were unable to have children so they adopted a boy. When the boy was 4 years of age, they adopted three girls— sisters age 4 years, 3 years, and 18 months. Howard and Nita treated all the children as equals and gave them a great deal of love and care. Those kids always addressed Nita as Honey. On April 19,

1992, Juanita Arline passed away at the age of 74. Her grateful and loving children openly wept at her funeral. Nita was interred next to her parents, grandfather, and sister at the Winona Community Cemetery.

Melvin Eugene was the final sibling to marry. He didn't marry right away. He probably realized that after his ordeals with the Nazis in Europe, he was not ready for a relationship. He was always a free spirit, and the imprisonment had taken a heavy toll on his mental well-being. Also, he had some unfinished business after the war. He went back to Oakesdale High School, completed his senior year, and graduated in 1946.

At first Mel seemed lost from his ordeal, but he gravitated toward Jack Elkins, the only other prison camp survivor in the small town of Oakesdale. Jack and Mel spent a great deal of time running around together. They were out to have fun and make up for lost time. As Jack explained it, "We never, ever discussed our war experiences seriously—we only joked about them and laughed about how each other could have gotten into such a predicament." Knowing that Mel had attended ski school, Jack queried, "How could you have the nerve to think you could ski right into a platoon of Nazis?"

Their time together was certainly cathartic, but they eventually stopped discussing prison camp altogether. At some point they only talked about their high school days, football, women, work, and the future. Jack shared with author Bob Wodnik, "It came over me like that, like a jolt. You drift back into civilization, but it didn't last very long. If you thought about it much, that is what would destroy you. You drive it out or you give up to it and let it destroy you." They drove it out, and neither Mel nor Jack discussed it unless questioned.

When Mel finished high school, he matriculated in an industrial technology program at Eastern Washington State College. After college Mel moved to Roseburg, Oregon, to be close to his sister, Nita, and her husband, Howard. Mel landed a position with PP&L Water Power Project at Toketee (Umpqua National Forest). It was during this work at Toketee that he learned the skills he would later use to establish the Mel Gregory Concrete Company.

Now that he was self-sufficient, on June 9, 1952, Mel married the beautiful young redhead who had caught his eye. Delma Deloris Fisher was known as Rusty. Rusty and Mel bought a mountainside overlooking Roseburg, and Mel built a beautiful, modern home on the spacious property.

In 1953 they had their first child, a girl, and 3 years later they had a boy. Mel discovered that he felt serene and confident when he was fishing. He spent a good deal of his time with family or friends, fishing the Umpqua River for salmon and steelhead. But one of his favorite fishing spots was deep in the high woods of Umpqua National Forest. Soda Springs was calm and loaded with rainbow trout and German brown trout. It provided splendid fishing, but more importantly it gave Mel the solitude that provided him peace of mind.

Mel was an industrious and adept concrete worker and company manager. With only one good eye and large, powerful arms, He earned the nickname of Popeye. Mel ran his company for 50 years and retired in 2000, but he continued to supervise home construction projects up until his final week. Melvin Eugene passed away on January 12, 2008 — 8 years after his semi-retirement and just two weeks short of his 83rd birthday. He was laid to rest on the 21st. The service was officiated by Pastor Vance Culpepper. The melodic tunes of Vince Gill's *Go Rest High Upon That Mountain* could be heard playing in the background. Mel's loving children took his ashes high into the Umpqua and scattered those remains at the tranquil Soda Springs.

Five of Pearl's children had survived to make a good living and raise families. If Pearl and Charles, Sr. could have looked into the future, they would have been proud of their children and their accomplishments. Back on the Winona farm, Pearl always knew they'd be successful—she always believed in her children.

Pearl Johnson Gregory, 1912.

Jack Elkins, the longtime family friend of the Gregory brothers, dealt with the trauma of his World War II experiences by commiserating with Mel and then Speck. He decided to push the pain and hate out and continue with his life. Jack became an award-winning automotive salesman for Stoddard-Wendle Ford in Spokane, Washington. He retired to the community of Everett, Washington. He wouldn't talk about his experiences for 50 years until author Bob Wodnik convinced him to provide a long series of interviews for the book, *Captured Honor*. Since then Jack has talked freely about his experiences during the war, and he enthusiastically enjoys sharing his memories of the Gregory family. He also proudly discusses his 16 grandchildren and great-grandchildren, including a young U.S. Marine Corps Captain. As of the writing of this book, Jack is experiencing health problems, some related to his early bouts of beriberi in the Philippines. But at age 91 he is alive in Everett, happy, contented with his life, and vividly lucid!

Fred Schuman, Mel Gregory's old friend from Garfield, was instrumental in buoying Mel's spirits while both young men were prisoners at Stalag 7A. Fred entered the service on December 15, 1943, and upon completion of his training at Ft. Benning, the young soldier was transferred to the 101st Airborne Division and sent to the European Theatre. After surviving his unit's bombing in England, Fred and the 101st parachuted into Holland (The Netherlands) and drove the Germans back. Subsequently, Fred was sent to France and became immersed in the Battle of the Bulge and helped to drive back the Germans and take back the village of Bastogne. Fred was wounded three times in the fighting and was eventually awarded with the Presidential Unit Citation and Purple Heart with Oak Leaf Cluster. The following was reported in the *Whitman County Enterprise,* Volume 59, Number 44, August 16, 1946:

> *During his army service, he was sole survivor in three cases where his companions were killed. In one case, an officer who was sitting beside him in a car was killed when they were caught in an enemy ambush. In another case, out of three in a foxhole, Fred was the only survivor when they became the target of the enemy guns. In England, he survived a bombing in which many persons lost their lives.*

Fred was liberated from Stalag 7A in late 1945 and settled back home in Garfield by mid-January, 1946. After all PFC John Frederick Schuman had been through, after all his near-death experiences, after his treatment as a prisoner of war—on August 14, 1946, the young hero crashed his automobile 2 miles north of Pullman on the Pullman-Palouse Highway. He had been returning from medical treatment for a painful back ailment—an ailment he originally received from parachuting into Europe. Sadly, the following day

Fred died at St. Ignatius Hospital in Colfax. He was interred at the Garfield Cemetery on Sunday the 18th, just 8 months after his return to Whitman County.

Nelson Quast and Ernest Loy — like Charles, their fellow 20th Pursuit Squadron, 24th Pursuit Group friend — survived the Battle of Bataan, the Bataan Death March, and 2½ years of Japanese prison camps on Luzon. Unlike their good friend, they also survived the *Hokusen Maru* hellship and another year of Imperial labor camps in China and Japan. After the Imperial surrender, Ernest and Nels were temporarily stranded at a mining camp on a small northern Japanese island. They had to walk several miles before they reached a train that they took to the closest harbor. Eventually they were taken by ship to Guam for recovery at the military hospital. When Ernest first came to the Philippines, he weighed 190 pounds on a 6-foot frame. During captivity his weight fell to 90 pounds. Starting at 160 pounds on a 5-foot, 9-inch frame, Nelson had fallen to 80 pounds. A month later, Nels and Ernie left Guam, embarking for the U.S. in late September, 1945, aboard the *U.S.S. Storm King*. The men arrived in San Francisco on October 18 and proceeded to Fairchild Air Force Base near Spokane. They were allowed to visit their friend's mother in Oakesdale, Washington, to complete a solemn promise. They spent the day commiserating with Pearl and answering her questions. She accepted their information and bravely asked for additional details. They spoke of his bravery in the attack on Clark Field and in the Battle of Bataan, his skilled accomplishments, and his will to survive. Ernest shared the story of their 8-day escape from the march and the painful return to the march. They told her of Charles's horrendous treatment, his maladies, and the details of his final burial at sea. She stoically thanked them and bravely asked if they could send her letters and give all the details in writing. They agreed and went their separate ways.

Nels returned to Kennewick to meet his brother and sister and visit the resting place of his parents, who had died during the war.

Nels returned to Fairchild Air Force Base and on October 30, 1945, he was discharged with several medals, including the Medal of Honor. Nels had nothing else to do, so he decided to accept Fran's offer and proceed to the Wenatchee Valley for hunting and fishing. Nels felt that the valley was quite beautiful—full of green hillsides and abundant fish and game. There was nothing to hold him in the arid sagebrush of Kennewick, so he decided to stay in the Wenatchee area. Nels worked for the U.S. Forest Service in the summers and filled a clerking position at a local general store in the small town of Entiat during the remainder of the year. He met and then dated a charming young lady, Edith Cozart, who had just graduated from high school, and they married in 1947. They had two children and built a beautiful house overlooking the Columbia River; Nels enjoyed taking his family fishing at the expansive river. After completing his promise to Charles, for 50 years Nels never discussed his World War II experiences. He eventually started to talk about those horrendous days. When he was asked to speak at a Veterans Day assembly at the local high school, he consented. He discovered that the experience lifted a heavy weight from his shoulders. Thereafter, he agreed to discuss his experiences with anyone who would listen. The final years of Nels' life were the best and most carefree, but regrettably, Nelson Herman Quast passed away at age 82, in 2001.

When Ernest left Oakesdale he was distraught. He found that it was very difficult for him to talk about his old friend, Charles, but he forged ahead and told Pearl everything. He openly wept during much of the time he spent with Pearl. He didn't know what direction his life would take, so he decided to stay in the Air Corps, or Air Force, as it became known in 1947. His sister and brothers were living in Spokane, so he visited them. The following day he reported back to Fairchild Air Force Base near Spokane and extended his service contract. An Air Force Psychiatrist talked to Ernest about his experiences. The man was visibly shaken by Ernest's descriptions of the events he had suffered. The psychiatrist was especially affected by Ernest's description of the Bataan Death March and the voyage of the *Hokusen Maru*. The young psychiatrist admitted Ernest to the hospital, where the officer observed and met with him daily. The officer was bothered by the extreme hatred shown for MacArthur, Roosevelt, and the Japanese, but he was most disturbed by Ernest's violent nightmares. His experiences had certainly taken a heavy toll on Ernest's body, mind, subconscious, and emotions. After months of treatment, the psychiatrist recommended the next step: Face the Japanese people and get to know them. Ernest agreed, and he was eventually reassigned to Japan. It worked! Ernest enjoyed himself in Tokyo and got to know everyday people. They were the polar opposite of the sadistic militarists he experienced on Luzon. Ernest was on his way to some semblance of a normal life.

After returning from Japan, Ernest was variously transferred to Fairchild Air Force Base, Grand Forks Air Force Base near Minot, North Dakota, and Davis-Monthan Air Force Base near Tucson, Arizona. When he returned to Spokane, Ernest married, fathered a daughter, and adopted a son. Wherever he was transferred, he managed to find the serenity of an isolated stream to fish. He often took his children along to enjoy the quiet solitude. Ernest retired from the Air Force in 1966 at the highest Non-Commissioned Officer rank of Chief Master Sergeant. He wanted to serve his community, so he became a Scout Master for the Boy Scouts. Ernest discovered that he had a great deal to offer children in camping, fishing, hiking, and general living experience. He eventually became an executive for the Scouts and served a total of 19 years for the organization. Ernie was honored with the Grey Wolf Award from the Tohono O'Odham Band (Desert People) for his diligent efforts to instruct the tribe's boys and young men.

Ernest used to take his children fishing north of Spokane near Chattaroy. They fished Little Spokane River for Eastern brook trout, Bear Creek for rainbow trout, and any of the small creeks in the area. He was at peace when fishing in these isolated locations. His daughter confided that he never talked about his late best friend,

Charles, or the events of the war. But he did talk about Francis Agnes, who had started a support group for POWs. Fran visited him often and buoyed Ernest's spirits. After the support groups and reunions, Ernest's nightmares seldom recurred. Before Ernest passed away, he had forgiven the Japanese and Roosevelt, but he never forgave and always held a deep resentment toward MacArthur. The end came for Chief Master Sergeant Ernest Harold Loy, USAF retired, on May 5, 2008. He had survived his three favorite buddies from the 20th Pursuit Squadron—Charlie, Nels, and Fran. Like Mel Gregory, Ernie had his ashes scattered at his favorite creek, the Palisades Creek located on Camp Lawton in Arizona—the Boy Scout Camp where Ernie found his serenity by helping others.

Francis Agnes continued in the Air Force until 1962. He was stationed at a number of air bases throughout the United States but spent several years at Fairchild Air Force Base near Spokane. He often fished in nearby lakes for relaxation. Fran eventually met, courted, and married Marlene Murie, his second wife. Before that marriage Fran had been married and divorced. He had three children from that first marriage; one was named Gregory, and we wonder if the name was inspired by his friendship with Charles, Jr. Francis Agnes often went back to Wenatchee to visit family, to fish, and visit his old friend Nelson Quast. After the service, Fran and Marlene lived in Spokane for several years and then moved to Everett, where he worked for the Washington State Employment Security Department for 20 years. Fran started a POW support group in Everett and traveled to meet with former POWs at Spokane, then throughout the Pacific Northwest, and ultimately throughout the United States. Fran was national president of the American Ex-POW group from 1990 to 1991. He also helped to organize annual Bataan Death March reunions, where he was always happy to see his old pal Ernie. His nightmares subsided. He helped to heal hundreds of tortured souls, but his altruistic support group efforts probably helped Fran most of all. Captain Francis Winifred Agnes, USAF retired, passed away February 9, 2003. He is interred at Tahoma

National Veteran's Cemetery near Kent, Washington. Fran and his Ex-POW support group helped establish the cemetery, which currently holds over 40,000 deceased veterans on 157 acres. Fran's wife, Marlene, said that she remembers Fran's reminiscing about his valiant friends on Bataan, and he always had a deep, abiding respect for their leader, General Jonathan Wainwright of Walla Walla, Washington. However, like so many other veterans of the Battle of Bataan, he despised both Roosevelt and MacArthur and never forgave them for their abandonment of the thousands of Americans who died in the Philippines.

Robert Goldsworthy from the Oakesdale-Rosalia area was a major in the 881st Squadron, 500th Bomb Group, 73rd Wing, U.S. Army Air Corps. On December 3, 1944, his *Rosalia Rocket* was shot down north of Tokyo, Japan, in the Chiba Prefecture, and Bob experienced horrendous conditions for 4 months at Kempei Tai Prison. During that time, he was on starvation rations and fell from 170 pounds down to 85 pounds, half his original weight. After Kempei, Bob was transferred on February 3, 1945, to Omori Prison Camp, where he languished until his liberation on August 29, 1945. Bob returned home, remained in the Air Corps for a year, and then transferred to the Air Force Reserves. Bob retired from the Air Force Reserves in 1975. Major General Robert F. Goldsworthy, USAFR retired, was a respected member of the Washington State House of Representatives for eight terms. He wrote the book, *Our Last Mission,* in 1948 and then in 2010, at the age of 93, Bob wrote a revised edition. *Our Last Mission* details his treatment at the hands of the Japanese militarists, as well as his efforts to connect positively with the Japanese people in later years. As of the writing of this book, Bob and his wife Jean are living in Spokane. Bob is healthy, talkative, and lucid at 96 years of age!

Sam Grashio, a captain in the 21st Pursuit Squadron, 24th Pursuit Group, stayed in the Air Force until 1965. He returned to his beloved Spokane, Washington, and his alma mater, Gonzaga University, to become an assistant to the Jesuit school's president. Sam retired from Gonzaga in 1977 and went on to write a book about his experiences in the Philippine Islands entitled *Return to Freedom*. His book, co-authored with Bernard Norling, was first published in 1982. In 1991 he was traveling via airline to Spokane from Los Angeles. Sam was returning from a reunion of his Pursuit Group pilots. At the same time, Delbert and Nina Gregory were returning from a China-Burma-India Hump Pilots Association reunion. Coincidentally, the two men were seated next to each other on the plane. Casual conversation led to reminiscing about World War II and eventually—Charles and the Bataan Death March and the prison camps. The two veterans ended up having a non-stop conversation for the entire trip. The encounter was surely cathartic for both of these older gentlemen, and one wonders how many thousands of chance encounters occurred like theirs—encounters of brave veterans sharing memories of experiences spanning the past 65 years. Approximately 2 years after that chance meeting of Sam and Del, Colonel Samuel C. Grashio, USAF retired, died in 1993.

Bob Mailheau, the 24th Pursuit Group flying infantryman from Hollywood, after surviving his escape from the death march, fought guerilla warfare on Luzon until the end of the struggle. He stayed in the newly formed Air Force until 1955. Bob moved to Palm Desert, California, and became a successful bank executive before retiring. As of this writing, at 92 years of age, he is talkative, lucid, informative, and happy in Palm Desert!

The human cost of World War II is incalculable. The anguish experienced by those back home waiting for loved ones, can never be fully grasped. The pain and helplessness experienced by Pearl can never be known. She was stoic and seldom allowed others to see her emotions, but she was in pain, and it certainly took a toll upon her health. Millions of other Americans felt the same pain, knowing the suffering experienced by their loved ones, but not knowing whether they would be able to return home. Death from war has never been unique. Mistreatment of prisoners during war is also not unique. But that is no comfort to those who have been affected by war.

The American military fatalities due to World War II totaled 416,800, over eight times as many deaths as World War I. Additionally, there were 9,500 merchant marine deaths, 1,900 Coast Guard deaths, and 1,700 civilian fatalities. The total death toll reached 418,500. The soldiers, sailors, Marines, and air corpsmen came from all walks of life and all occupations. They came from the countryside and they came from every imaginable size of community, but the largest percentage came from small towns and farm communities just like Oakesdale.

In 1940 the total population of Oakesdale was 590. A total of 93 young men from Oakesdale served in the armed forces during World War II. Like Mel, a few of them were a mere 17 years of age. Also, like Mel, 48 of them served in the Army; and 24 were in the Navy. Charles, Speck, Delbert, and 12 others served in the Air Corps. Three were Navy Seabees. One member was in the Coast Guard. The U.S. Marine Corps accepted the proud Jack Elkins and Boyd Henning. Like the Gregorys, some families sent more than one young man into the service of their country. Those Oakesdale mothers sending two sons included the families of Barber, Clark, Eagle, Ellis, Greer, Gunn, Haire, Hubner, Litzenburger, Robinson, Sienknicht, and Walker. Families sending three brothers included those of DeVaney, Hanford, Henning, Reel, and Stanzack. The Gregory family was the only one to send four brothers. The following article appeared in the *Spokane Chronicle* March 20, 1943:

> **BROTHERS**: *Four sons of Mrs. Pearl Gregory of Oakesdale are in the service – two overseas and two in the United States. Left to right, with the oldest first, the boys are; Private Charles R. Gregory, a*

prisoner of the Japanese, held in the Philippine islands since April, 1942; Technical Sergeant Donald F. Gregory, a B-17 Flying Fortress gunner in North Africa; Private First Class Delbert E. Gregory, Marana, Ariz., and Melvin E. Gregory, Camp Hale, Colo. Sergeant Gregory, recipient of the Air Medal with 11 Oak Leaf clusters, recently completed 50 missions in aerial combat against the enemy.

Realistically, with four sons in the armed forces, the odds that one of Pearl's boys would experience death or prisoner status were high, but of course that statistic would have been no comfort to her.

Three young Oakesdale men became prisoners of war: Jack Elkins, Mel Gregory, and Charles Ralph Gregory, Jr. One young man, Fred Schuman, from nearby Garfield, was a prisoner of war. Fred was held along with Mel Gregory in Stalag 7A. Also, a young farmer from McCoy Valley, near Rosalia and Oakesdale, was Major Robert F. Goldsworthy, the pilot of a B-29 Super Fortress of the 881st Squadron. His *Rosalia Rocket* was shot down between Tokyo and Yokohama. Like Mel Gregory and Jack Elkins, both Fred Schuman and Bob Goldsworthy survived and returned home.

Of the 93 Oakesdale boys, there were 9 who paid the ultimate price: Melvin Morse, Norman Phillips, Howard Hanford, Carroll Waddell, Benjamin Billingsley, Donald Lindsay, Clyde Danielson, Delbert Eugene Miller, and Charles Ralph Gregory, Jr.

According to author Malcolm Decker's research, only 103 American soldiers had escaped the Bataan Death March. At war's end, 30 of those soldiers, like Bob Mailheau and Sam Grashio, remained guerillas at liberty; 6 of the escapees were unaccounted for; 29, among them Ernest Harold Loy, were recaptured and were still prisoners at war's end; and 38 others, among them Charles Ralph Gregory, Jr., had been recaptured and died in captivity.

Many German Nazis committed horrendous war crimes toward millions of Jewish civilians, as well as many Gypsies, Serbs, Czechs, Slovenes, Slovaks, Russians, Poles, and other Slavs. However, unlike their Japanese allies, most of the Germans honored the Geneva Convention, at least when it came to American prisoners of war.

Although 4% of American prisoners died in German captivity, a much higher percentage of American prisoners of war died under the control of the Imperial Japanese militarists. The Japanese took American prisoners throughout Asia and the Pacific. Of all the American prisoners taken by the Japanese, 27% died in captivity. Yet, of all the troops, American and Filipino, under the American flag—all these abandoned soldiers who had surrendered at Bataan— 65% died in Japanese captivity. One of those soldiers was Charles Ralph Gregory, Jr.

Ruth Haire and Donald Gregory
agreed to marry December 1,
1943.

Nina Littleton and Delbert Gregory
married April 1, 1945.

Delma "Rusty" Fisher and Melvin Eugene Gregory married
June 9, 1952. Photo taken 1953.

Mildred and Chester Gregory
wedded November 23, 1941.
Photo taken 1943.

Howard Long and Juanita Gregory
wedded May 1, 1945.

Epilogue

Finishing the Vigil

*There is a sacredness in tears. They are not the mark of weakness,
but of power. They speak more eloquently than ten thousand
tongues. They are messengers of overwhelming grief…
and unspeakable love.*

— Washington Irving

That's the story of Neva and her very short, yet joyful life—the story of her mother and her mother's anguish—the story of her industrious father and his short life, the story of her brother Charles, Jr.'s short life and horrendous treatment, and yes, the story of her other four brothers and the sister who never knew her. Neva had missed a lot of life, but what had the world missed in her? What had Whitman County and the entirety of its people missed—if only that sweet little girl with a happy countenance had survived?

And there we were with the swirling, dust-laden wind, almost a century after Neva's birth, 97 years after her death, my son, my eldest granddaughter, and my father, in the family section of the Winona cemetery. There we stood—to honor Neva. I had read a few months earlier in the Whitman County Library that the name *Winona* originated with the Santee Tribe of Native Americans from the area of Minnesota. It means *first-born daughter*. And ironically for her parents, Pearl and Charles, Sr., Neva was their first-born daughter, who was born in Winona and died 2 years later.

I used a spade to clear away a trench for the headstone. The wind picked up, and dust swirled around us and got into our eyes.

My dad and I began to place the stone marker in the trench. Delbert snapped at me, "I'll do it!" Once he had the stone in place, my son, Trevor, then opened his bible and solemnly read from Revelations 21:4, "And God shall wipe all tears from their eyes; and there shall be no more death, neither sorrow, nor crying, neither shall there be pain: for the former things are passed away." We stood in silence, uncertain of what to do or what to say. Trevor and his daughter Madeline walked back to the Jeep to get out of the dusty gusts of wind. My father and I pushed the powdery soil against the stone to fill in the trench around it. As I stood, he remained on his knees and looked away from me. But I could see tears rolling down the side of his face. I could see tears on the ground.

I had seen him cry only once before, in Lakewood General Hospital, Tacoma, Washington, when he threw himself across the foot of my younger sister's bed and bawled. That was almost as shocking to me as the car accident we had just survived an hour earlier.

We had been coming back from the 1962 World's Fair as King County Sheriff's Deputy Larry Robinson was recklessly speeding to the scene of a minor accident. A young lady had fallen and sprained her ankle. Attempting to be the first one on the scene, the impatient deputy tried to pass a car on the inside of the narrow Golden Given Roadway. He lost control of his patrol car, hit the ditch, overcorrected, crossed the dividing line, and collided into us at a high speed! Our Plymouth station wagon was shredded. On June 15, *The Tacoma News Tribune* stated, "Officers at the scene remarked that it was a miracle no lives were lost." We were all injured, but my younger sister bore the worst of it. She had internal injuries, a crushed pelvis, and numerous deep gashes on her face and throughout her body. She was badly disfigured. She survived, but due to the internal injuries, she was never able to have children. Christina Jean was a beautiful little girl who had won 3rd place in the Northwest Inland Empire Children's Photo Contest. Delbert was devastated that his little daughter's life was so drastically changed for the worse… so quickly and so violently.

Then Delbert had cried for his daughter... and now he cried again. Was he crying for the sister he never knew? Were the tears for the father and grandfather who left this world when he was so very young, for the big brother who helped to raise him — the one who had spent 3 years abandoned in hell and who had died under the torturous conditions of the Japanese Imperial Forces? Perhaps he was remembering the younger brother he had helped raise — the one who was severely injured and held prisoner by the Nazis for over 13 months. Was he crying for the mother who had worked so hard to help her children and yet died of cancer at 52 years of age? Was he remembering his closest brother, Speck, the person he most respected in life, the man with whom he had spent so many years hunting and fishing right up until Speck's death 3 years previous? Possibly he was thinking of the struggle on this very land, or the struggle through The Great Depression. Perhaps he was remembering all the happy moments with friends and family and realizing they were all gone now — classmates, friends, brothers, and sisters, and now the final stone laid for the first of his siblings, Neva.

And now, Delbert's tears rushed down his face and disappeared, absorbed by the dry, powdery soil — the same soil that his father had worked so hard, 14 hours a day, to raise a crop and provide for the family. The strong wind dried the tears on Delbert's cheeks, but left them dust stained. The tears on the ground vanished. The soil that had promised life over a century ago drank up the tears as I helped him stand. The soil was dry again... no more tears....

ACKNOWLEDGMENTS

First of all I must thank my parents, Delbert and Nina Gregory, for keeping copious amounts of photographs and printed material over all these years. As a curious child of 10, I first became interested in the events of United States history, especially homesteading, The Great Depression, and World War II. The impetus for this interest came from the discovery of material in my parents' dresser. There I found photographs, letters, postcards, military awards, souvenirs, telegrams, and documents. Much of it was unbelievable to me at that age. But as I grew up, I asked many questions about those events. When I asked questions of my father that pertained to those subjects, he would grudgingly give some information. Occasionally, he would give me more details than I could comprehend, and I wouldn't bring it up for weeks or even months. Some of the war-related information was too brutal and inhumane to be credible.

However, as I listened to stories repeated from Delbert and his siblings, I came to realize that they shared the same memories, both joyous and deleterious. Then I began researching and discovered that no matter how much I delved into the subjects, all the stories were reinforced. I had always felt that their story should be told, but I never seriously considered writing it myself until after I had retired from teaching.

Delbert Gregory is the primary source of information for the entire book, with the exception of Chapter 3, although we have discussed those geological events many times. Almost all events in this book were part of the oral history I heard throughout my childhood and leading up to the present day. Delbert's memory has always been keen. He painted with a broad brush and yet gave minute and exact details as well. Once I started the writing, I spoke to him every day; he continued to provide me with more precise details and additional memories and anecdotes. His astute attention to detail and trivia was extremely beneficial. All the stories were corroborated by my father's siblings or by letters, documents, telegrams, postcards, and historical writings and books. The time I spent with Delbert since my retirement has been informative and, more importantly, it has brought us closer together.

I wish to acknowledge the contributions of Pearl Gregory and Charles Gregory, Jr. and their many letters, photographs, and documents. Since they both died shortly before my birth, the study of those primary sources brought me closer to them. Additionally, the oral history from Don "Speck" Gregory, Mel Gregory, Chet Gregory, and Nita Long was supportive of Delbert's stories and my research. Special emphasis is given to Speck. During the past 50 years, I spent a good deal of time bird hunting and fishing with him and my father. It was enlightening to listen to the two of them reminisce about their childhoods, their brothers, the letters from Charles, Jr., and their years in the service of our great nation.

For additional supporting contributions I would like to thank cousins of the Menzie family, including Norman, John, Jeff, and Dan, as well as my first cousins Donald Steven Gregory, Stephen Phillip Gregory, Linda Haladyna, and Terry Leibenguth.

I would like to thank the families of the late Nelson H. Quast, Ernest H. Loy, and Francis W. Agnes for those men's friendship, assistance, and care of my uncle during their equally horrendous ordeals on Luzon and the *Hokusen Maru*. I would also like to recognize Nels and Ernie for the information that they provided to my grandmother. I thank Mike Loy for the information that he provided me about Ernest Loy's years after the war. I thank Lanny Quast for the information of Nelson's early years, mining labor camp, and post-war years. I am extremely grateful to Harolene Loy Swenson for her frank and informative accounts of her father's post-war years. I appreciate the abundance of contributions from Lou Schuman, Fred's sister-in-law. Also, I am grateful for the extensive and detailed information provided by Marlene Agnes, Fran's widow.

I thank Leslie Lamb for allowing me to explore the old homestead and size up the property. As I took photos of the farm, its varied topography, and rusty machinery from the era of my grandfather and great-grandfather, the experience transported me back in time. That helped me feel closer to the land and to those hopeful, industrious farmers who once tilled the soil.

I acknowledge the help of the Entiat Community Historical Society and its secretary, Phyllis Griffith, for providing me with supporting information about Nelson Quast and his interviews with the *Entiat Valley Explorer*. I would like to thank Sam Grashio, Jr. for providing me with memories of Captain Samuel Grashio. I would also like to thank Bob Mailheau and Jack Elkins for personally sharing memories with me. Jack especially was instrumental in providing his memories of Oakesdale and the five Gregory brothers, his closest friends: Charlie, Speck, Chet, Del, and Mel.

Finally, I acknowledge the contributions of my supportive son Trevor Eugene Gregory. And I especially recognize and appreciate the support and paramount patience of my loving wife, Kathy Marie Sloan Gregory.

SELECTED BIBLIOGRAPHY

Alt, David. *Glacial Lake Missoula and Its Humongous Floods*. Missoula, MT: Mountain Press Publishing Company, 2001.

Boorstin, Daniel J., and Brooks Mather Kelley. *A History of the United States*. Englewood Cliffs, NJ: Prentice-Hall, Inc., 1990.

Bradley, James. *Flyboys*. New York: Little, Brown and Company, 2003.

Cowman, Lettie B. *Streams in the Desert*. Los Angeles, CA: The Oriental Missionary Society, 1937.

Goldsworthy, Robert F. *Our Last Mission*. Martinsville, IN: Fideli Publishing, 2010.

Grashio, Samuel C., and Bernard Norling. *Return to Freedom*. Tulsa, OK: MCN Press, 1982.

Gress, Robert. *Milkrun*. Merrick, NY: Cross-Cultural Communications, 1995.

Hastings, Max. *Inferno: The World at War, 1939–1945*. New York: Vintage Books, 2011.

Johansen, Dorothy O., and Charles M. Gates. *Empire of the Columbia: A History of the Pacific Northwest*. New York: Harper & Row, Publishers, Inc., 1967.

Kjack, Jeanne. *Window to the Palouse*. Spokane, WA: A. J Kjack, 1998.

Martin, John G. *It Began at Imphal: The Combat Cargo Story*. Athens, OH: The Lawhead Press, 1988.

McLynn, Frank. *The Burma Campaign: Disaster into Triumph 1942–45*. New Haven, CT: Yale University Press, 2011.

Norman, Michael, and Elizabeth M. Norman. *Tears in the Darkness: The Story of the Bataan Death March and Its Aftermath*. New York: Picador, 2009.

Ortega, Abel, Jr. *Courage on Bataan and Beyond*. Bloomington, IN: Author House Publishing, 2005.

Pelz, Ruth. *The Washington Story: A History of Our State*. Seattle, WA: Seattle Public Schools, 1979.

Raban, Jonathan. *Bad Land: An American Romance*. New York: Pantheon Books, 1996.

Sledge, E. B. *With the Old Breed*. New York: Ballantine Books, 1981.

Spencer, Otha C. *Flying the Hump: Memories of an Air War*. College Station, TX: Texas A & M University Press, 1994.

Stewart, Sydney. *Give Us This Day*. London, England: Staples Press Limited, 1957.

Welch, Bob. *Resolve: From the Jungles of WW II Bataan, the Epic Story of a Soldier, a Flag, and a Promise Kept*. New York: Berkley Books, 2012.

Willett, Gaylen. "Entiatite Nelson Quast, Former POW, Recalls 1942's Bataan Death March." *Entiat Valley Explorer*, January 28, 1998, pp. 1-3.

Wodnik, Bob. *Captured Honor: POW Survival in the Philippines and Japan*. Pullman, WA: Washington State University Press, 2003.

INTERNET WEB SITES

http://aad.archives.gov

http://bataanmissing.com/pages/completebilibidrosterv.htm

http://www.battlingbastardsbataan.com (maintained by Fred Baldasarre)

http://www.mansell.com/pow-index.html

http://en.wikipedia.org/wiki/world_war_II_casualties

http://www.philippine-defenders.lib.wv.us

http://research.archives.gov

http://west-point.org/family/japanese-pow/rosters.htm

Primary Sources

Agnes, Marlene. Transcribed telephonic interviews, reminiscences, copies of letters, postcards, and documents, March–April 2013.

Elkins, Jack. Transcribed telephonic interviews, March 2013.

Goldsworthy, Robert F., Sr. Transcribed telephonic interviews, March 2013.

Grashio, Samuel, Jr. Transcribed telephonic interview, February 2013.

Gregory, Charles R., Jr., Postcards, letters, and telegram, September 18, 1940 – December 9, 1941.

Gregory, Chester E. Oral history, 1958–1990.

Gregory, Delbert E. Oral history, 1956–2013; transcribed interviews, 2011–2013; personal collection of photographs, newspaper clippings, documents, awards, certificates, letters, postcards, souvenirs, and telegrams, 1912–2012; Oaken Script school annuals, 1934–1944, Sustineo Alas Scott Field Yearbook, 1944; CBI Hump Pilots Association newsletters, 1986–2008.

Gregory, Donald F. Oral history, 1957–2009; personal collection of photographs, newspaper clippings, awards, letters, and documents, 1927–2009.

Gregory, D. Steven. Transcribed interviews, 2011–2013; personal collection of photographs, letters, newspaper clippings, and documents, 1927–2013.

Gregory, Melvin E. Oral history, 1959–1984; personal prison camp memoirs, letters, photographs, postcards, documents, and military records, 1910–2008.

Gregory, Nina L. Oral history, 1956–2013; photographs, 1942–44; transcribed interviews, 2011–2013.

Gregory, Pearl. Personal collection of photographs, newspaper clippings, postcards, letters, documents, report cards, legal papers, and telegrams, 1912–1946.

Gregory, Stephen P. Transcribed telephonic interviews, texts, and copied e-mails, February–April, 2013; personal collection of documents, newspaper clippings, photographs, letters, awards, postcards, and journal, 1910–2008.

Haladyna, Linda. Transcribed telephonic interviews, 2012–2013; photos, 1939–1946.

Leibenguth, Terry. Transcribed telephonic interviews and copied e-mails, 2012–2013.

Long, Juanita A. Oral history, 1959–1991.

Loy, Ernest H. Letters and newspaper clippings, 1945–1946.

Loy, Mike. Transcribed telephonic interviews, March 2013.

Loy-Swenson, Harolene. Transcribed series of telephonic interviews, texts, and e-mails, March–April 2013; photos, 1935–1990.

Mailheau, Bob. Transcribed telephonic interviews, December 2012.

Menzie, Dan. Transcribed telephonic interviews, December 2012.

Menzie, Jeff. Transcribed telephonic interviews, October 2012.

Menzie, John. Transcribed telephonic interviews, January 2013.

Menzie, Norman. Transcribed telephonic interviews, November 2012.

Quast, Lanny. Transcribed telephonic interviews and e-mails, April 2013.

Quast, Nelson H. Collection of letters, 1945–1946; transcribed interviews, 1998.

Schuman, Lou. Transcribed personal interviews, April 2013; letters, newspaper articles, and obituary, 1943–1965.

INDEX

ABOUT THE AUTHOR

Christopher Eugene Gregory served in the U.S. Marine Corps during the Vietnam era and used the G.I. Bill to help obtain his education. He earned his B.A.Ed. degree and social science teaching credential in 1973 at Central Washington University. During his matriculation there, he was inducted into Kappa Delta Pi International Honor Society in Education. In 1997, he earned his M.Ed. and principal's credential at Heritage University and, 5 years later, in 2002, earned his superintendent's credential at Washington State University. Chris served as keynote speaker for several graduation ceremonies and coached basketball for 26 years. He retired after 34 years as a history and geography teacher and administrator in small schools in eastern Washington. Chris enjoys pheasant hunting, fly tying, and fishing. He lives with Kathy Marie, his wife of 43 years, on Tekoa Mountain, northern Whitman County, Washington State.

CPSIA information can be obtained at www.ICGtesting.com
Printed in the USA
LVOW08s1426030515

437053LV00010B/630/P